CHIN ...E

VEGETARIAN MINI SPRING ROLLS

Preparation time: 35 minutes
Cooking time: 30 minutes
Makes 20

4 dried Chinese mushrooms
150 g fried bean curd
1 tablespoon oil
1 teaspoon crushed garlic
¾ teaspoon finely grated ginger
6 spring onions, finely chopped
3 cups shredded Chinese
  cabbage
1 large carrot, grated
1 tablespoon soy sauce
5 large spring roll wrappers
oil for deep-frying

➤ SOAK MUSHROOMS in hot water to cover for 30 minutes. Drain, squeeze to remove excess liquid. Remove stems and chop caps finely. Cut the bean curd into small cubes and set aside.

1 Heat oil in a wok or heavy-based frying pan, swirling gently to coat the base and side. Add the garlic, ginger, spring onion, cabbage, carrot, mushrooms and bean curd.
Stir-fry for 5 minutes over a moderate to high heat until the vegetables are softened. Add the soy and stir to combine. Cool.

2 Cut each spring roll wrapper into four squares. Work with one square at a time, keeping the remainder covered with a clean, damp tea-towel.

Place 2 teaspoons of the filling on the wrapper and fold one point over. Fold in the two side points, then roll up towards the last point, forming a log shape. Seal point with a little flour and water paste. Repeat with remaining wrappers and filling.

3 Heat the extra oil in a wok and deep-fry the rolls, four at a time, until golden, about 3 minutes. Drain rolls on absorbent paper. Serve warm.

COOK'S FILE

Storage time: Prepare rolls ready for frying 1 day ahead. They can also be stored uncooked in the freezer for up to 1 month. Deep-fry from frozen in moderately hot oil for 5 minutes.

Variation: Mini spring rolls are more appetising than large, but, if you find them too time-consuming to make, halve the preparation time by using whole wrappers and double the amount of filling for each roll. Deep-fry for 5 minutes.

Hint: Large spring roll wrappers are sold in 250 g packets, 215 mm square, which contain 20 wrappers.
For Chinese cooking, peanut oil is the preferred oil for both stir-frying and deep-frying. Its flavour is mild and does not overpower other ingredients. It can also be heated without smoking to the high temperature required for deep-frying. Cool and strain after use to remove food particles. Store in an airtight container in the refrigerator. Use for a maximum of two fryings only; then discard.

1   2   3

MINI SPRING ROLLS

Preparation time: 45 minutes
Cooking time: 25 minutes
Makes 20

4 dried Chinese mushrooms
3 cups finely shredded Chinese
  cabbage
2 teaspoons salt
6 teaspoons oil
½ teaspoon crushed garlic
1 teaspoon grated ginger
150 g pork mince
¼ teaspoon ground black
  pepper
1 tablespoon soy sauce
1 tablespoon oyster sauce
2 large carrots, grated
3 teaspoons cornflour
2 tablespoons water
10 large spring roll wrappers
oil for deep-frying

➤ SOAK MUSHROOMS in hot water
to cover for 30 minutes. Drain, squeeze
to remove excess liquid. Remove stems
and chop the caps finely.
Place the Chinese cabbage in a
colander, sprinkle with salt and leave
for 10 minutes to draw out the excess
liquid. Rinse under cold, running
water, squeezing to remove as much
liquid as possible.

1 Heat oil in a wok or heavy-based
frying pan, swirling gently to coat
base and side. Add garlic and ginger
and cook until pale golden.
Increase heat to high, add mince and
stir-fry, breaking up any lumps, until
the meat changes colour. Add pepper,
soy and oyster sauces, stir through.
Add mushrooms, cabbage and carrot
and continue stir-frying for 3 minutes.
Mix cornflour with water and add to
meat mixture. Cook, stirring, until the
liquid is clear and thick. Leave to cool.

2 Cut spring roll wrappers diagonally
in half. Work with one triangle at a
time, keeping remainder covered with
a clean, damp tea-towel to prevent
them drying out.
Place 2 teaspoonfuls of the filling on a
triangle. Fold in the two side points,
then roll up towards the last point,
forming a log shape. Seal the point
with a little flour and water paste.
Repeat the procedure with remaining
wrappers and filling.

3 Heat the oil in a wok and deep-fry
the rolls, four at a time, until golden,
about 3 minutes. Drain on absorbent
paper. Serve warm with a sweet and
sour sauce.

COOK'S FILE

Storage time: Prepare rolls ready for
frying 1 day ahead; refrigerate. Can also
be stored uncooked in the freezer for up
to 1 month. Deep-fry from frozen in
moderately hot oil for 5 minutes.

1

2

3

STUFFED CAPSICUM WITH OYSTER SAUCE

Preparation time: 15 minutes
Cooking time: 15 minutes
Serves 4

125 g raw prawn meat, finely
    chopped
300 g lean pork mince
1 teaspoon salt
3 spring onions, finely chopped
3 tablespoons finely chopped
    water chestnuts
3 teaspoons soy sauce
2 teaspoons dry sherry
2 medium red capsicum
2 medium green capsicum
2 tablespoons oil
1 teaspoon finely chopped
    garlic
½ teaspoon finely grated ginger

Sauce
1 teaspoon cornflour
1 tablespoon oyster sauce
½ cup chicken stock

➤ THOROUGHLY COMBINE prawn
meat, pork, salt, spring onion, water
chestnuts, soy and sherry.

1 Cut each capsicum lengthways into
three or four segments. Remove the
seeds and thick membranes.

2 Fill the capsicum wedges with
mince mixture; cut in half.
Heat 1 tablespoon of the oil in a wok
or a heavy-based frying pan. Swirl
gently to coat base and side. Add
about half the capsicum pieces, meat
side down, and cook on medium to
high heat for 3 minutes on both sides
until cooked. Transfer to a plate, cover
and keep warm.

3 Repeat the cooking procedure with
remaining pieces. The exact cooking
time will depend on the thickness of
the filling.

To make Sauce: Mix all the sauce
ingredients until the cornflour has dissolved. Add garlic, ginger and sauce
mixture to the wok. Bring to the boil,
stirring gently. Reduce to a simmer,
cook for 1 minute or until the sauce
thickens. Serve capsicum pieces on a
platter with the sauce poured over.

COOK'S FILE

Storage time: The capsicum can be
prepared a few hours ahead up to the
cooking stage; refrigerate.

Variation: For a more lively sauce,
substitute 2 teaspoons of Chinese hot
bean sauce (see page 4), for the oyster
sauce. Or, add 2 teaspoons chilli sauce
to the sauce mixture.

Hint: Cornflour becomes translucent
in a sauce; wheat flour remains opaque
and is visually less appealing.

1

2

3

STEAMED PRAWN DUMPLINGS

Preparation time: 1 hour
Cooking time: 15 minutes
Makes 16

Dumplings
2¼ cups plain flour
1 tablespoon tapioca flour
1 tablespoon baking powder
2 teaspoons caster sugar
70 g lard, chopped
¾ cup warm water

Filling
250 g raw prawn meat
2 tablespoons finely chopped
   pork or ham fat
1 tablespoon soy sauce
2 teaspoons dry sherry
1 teaspoon sesame oil
2 spring onions, white part
   only, finely chopped
3 tablespoons finely chopped
   bamboo shoots

Dipping Sauce
3 tablespoons peanut oil
1 teaspoon minced fresh garlic
2 teaspoons finely chopped
   dried chilli or chilli flakes
1 tablespoon soy sauce,
   preferably dark
1 teaspoon lemon juice
1 teaspoon sesame paste, optional

➤ SIFT FLOURS, baking powder
and sugar in a medium bowl.

1 To make Filling: Chop the prawn
meat. Combine in a bowl with pork fat,
soy, sherry, sesame oil, spring onion
and bamboo shoots.

2 To make the Dumplings: Using
fingertips, rub the lard into the sifted
flour and sugar until the mixture
resembles coarse breadcrumbs.

3 Make a well in the centre. Add the
water, stir until mixture begins to
come together. Turn the dough onto a
lightly floured surface. Knead. Cover,
leave dough to rest for 15 minutes.
Divide dough into 16 equal portions.
Roll each portion into a small ball.

4 On a lightly floured surface, roll the
balls into circles of 10 cm diameter.
Place 1 heaped teaspoon of the filling
in the centre of each circle. Brush
edges with water.

5 Pinch the edges together to seal.

6 Half fill a wok with water, cover
and bring to the boil. Place dumplings
on a lined and oiled bamboo steamer
rack, place rack over the boiling water.
Cover, steam for 12 minutes. Carefully
remove dumplings to a serving plate.
serve with the Dipping Sauce.

To make Dipping Sauce: Heat the
oil in a small pan and cook the garlic
until it is on the verge of colouring;
add the chilli. When garlic is golden,
add the soy, lemon juice and sesame
paste, if using. Cool. Pour into small
dishes to serve.

COOK'S FILE

Storage time: Filling can be made up
to 1 day ahead, and Dipping Sauce up
to 2 days ahead. Store, covered, in the
refrigerator.

Hint: Use the Dipping Sauce also as a
general seasoning for a variety of rice
and noodle dishes. Make without the
sesame paste, if preferred.

Pork or ham fat can be purchased
from your butcher.

The traditional method of making soy
sauce has remained much the same for
centuries. Fermented soybeans and
roasted grain (wheat or barley) are
combined and injected with yeast. They
are salted and left to mature in vats.
Quicker methods use flavourings that
give a less intense flavour. For quality,
look for the word 'brewed' on the label.

1

2

3

4

5

6

WON TON SOUP

Preparation time: 40 minutes
Cooking time: 5 minutes
Serves 6

4 dried Chinese mushrooms
250 g pork mince
125 g raw prawn meat, finely
    chopped
1 teaspoon salt
1 tablespoon soy sauce
1 teaspoon sesame oil
2 spring onions, finely chopped
1 teaspoon grated ginger
2 tablespoons finely sliced
    water chestnuts
1 x 250 g packet won ton
    wrappers

5 cups chicken or beef stock
4 spring onions, very finely
    sliced, for garnish

➤ SOAK MUSHROOMS in hot water
to cover for 30 minutes. Drain, squeeze
to remove excess liquid. Remove stems
and chop the caps finely. Thoroughly
combine the mushrooms, pork, prawn
meat, salt, soy, sesame oil, spring
onion, ginger and water chestnuts.
1 Work with one won ton wrapper at
a time, keeping the remainder covered
with a clean, damp tea-towel to
prevent them drying out. Place heaped
teaspoonfuls of mince mixture on the
centre of each square.
2 Moisten the edges of the pastry,
fold in half diagonally and bring the
two points together. Place on a plate

dusted with flour to prevent sticking.
3 Cook won tons in rapidly boiling
water for 4 to 5 minutes.
Bring stock to the boil in a separate
pan. Remove won tons from water
with a slotted spoon and place in a
serving bowl. Garnish with the extra
spring onion and pour the simmering
stock over. Serve immediately.

COOK'S FILE

Storage time: The won tons can be
prepared 1 day ahead up to Step 3.
Place, covered, in the refrigerator.
Cook just before serving.
Variation: The filling ingredients can
be varied to include other seafood or
types of mince.
Hint: A 250 g packet of won ton
wrappers contains 60 small sheets.

1

2

3

CHICKEN AND SWEETCORN SOUP

Preparation time: 15 minutes
Cooking time: 10 minutes
Serves 4

200 g chicken breast fillets
1 teaspoon salt
2 egg whites
3 cups chicken stock,
    preferably homemade
1 cup creamed corn

1 tablespoon cornflour
2 teaspoons soy sauce
2 spring onions, diagonally
    sliced

➤ WASH CHICKEN under cold
water. Pat dry with absorbent paper.
Place in food processor bowl; process
until smooth. Add salt.
1 Lightly beat the egg whites in a
small bowl until foamy. Fold the egg
whites into the chicken mince.
2 Bring chicken stock to the boil and
add the creamed corn. Dissolve the

cornflour in a little water and add to
the soup, stirring until mixture thickens.
3 Reduce heat and add the chicken
mixture, breaking it up with a whisk.
Allow to heat through, without boiling,
for about 3 minutes. Season to taste with
soy. Serve sprinkled with the sliced
spring onion.

COOK'S FILE

Storage time: Cook this dish just
before serving.
Hint: Homemade chicken stock can be
frozen ready for use at any time.

1

3

Opposite: Won Ton Soup (top),
Chicken and Sweetcorn Soup (bottom).

SAN CHOY BAU

Preparation time: I hour
Cooking time: 10 minutes
Serves 4

8 dried Chinese mushrooms
1 small iceberg lettuce, washed
  and dried
500 g chicken mince
1 tablespoon soy sauce
1 tablespoon oil
¼ cup pine nuts
1 teaspoon minced garlic
4 spring onions, white part
  only, finely chopped
10 water chestnuts, chopped

Sauce
3 teaspoons caster sugar
1 tablespoon bean paste
3 teaspoons cornflour
1 tablespoon oyster sauce
½ cup water or chicken stock,
  preferably homemade

➤ SOAK MUSHROOMS in hot water to cover for 30 minutes. Drain, squeeze to remove the excess liquid.

1 Remove stems and slice caps finely. Refrigerate the lettuce to crisp it. Place chicken mince in a bowl, stir in soy.

2 Heat the oil in a wok, add nuts and cook over moderate heat until golden. Drain on absorbent paper. Add garlic to wok and cook gently until pale gold. Stir in spring onion. Add the chicken and cook over high heat, breaking up any lumps, for about 5 minutes or until thoroughly cooked. Stir the mixture occasionally. Add water chestnuts and mushrooms; cook 1 minute.

3 **To make Sauce:** Whisk all sauce ingredients together to dissolve sugar and cornflour. Make a well in the centre of chicken mixture and add the sauce mixture, stirring until it comes to the boil and thickens. Transfer to a serving bowl.

4 Separate lettuce leaves, place in individual serving bowls. Place chicken on a separate dish; garnish with nuts.

Each diner fills their lettuce leaf with chicken mixture, wrapping the lettuce around to make a package to hold with their fingers.

COOK'S FILE

Storage time: Cook this dish just before serving.

Hint: There are numerous types of bean paste, varying in colour and intensity of flavour. Experiment until you find one of the piquancy you like.

STEAMED BEEF BALLS IN LONG SOUP

Preparation time: 1 hour
Cooking time: 20 minutes
Serves 6

500 g lean beef mince
2 egg whites, lightly beaten
1 tablespoon iced water
2 tablespoons soy sauce
1 teaspoon sesame oil
2 teaspoons cornflour
2 tablespoons finely chopped
   fresh coriander
2 spring onions, finely chopped
1/4 teaspoon ground white
   pepper

1/4 teaspoon five spice
   powder

Long Soup
4 cups beef stock, preferably
   homemade
2 cups assorted Chinese
   vegetables, sliced very finely
   for rapid cooking
375 g fresh, thin egg noodles,
   cooked

➤ PLACE SMALL BATCHES of mince in a food processor bowl.
1 Using the pulse action, press button for 30 seconds or until mixture is a fine paste. Transfer to a bowl and add the remaining ingredients.
2 Roll level tablespoonfuls of mixture

into balls with wet hands. Half-fill a wok with water, cover, bring to the boil. Place mince balls in a steamer lined with lightly oiled greaseproof paper over the boiling water. Cover, steam for 20 minutes.
3 To make Long Soup: Bring stock to the boil in a separate pan, add the vegetables, cook 2 minutes. Pour into a tureen, add noodles and beef balls.

COOK'S FILE

Storage time: Beef balls can be made 1 day ahead and reheated in the boiling stock just before serving.
Variation: For Combination Long Soup, add 125 g each of peeled, cooked prawns, sliced barbecued pork and cooked chicken.

MARBLED SOY EGGS

Preparation time: 5 minutes
Cooking time: 15 minutes
Makes 6

6 eggs
½ cup soy sauce
½ cup water
1 star anise
2 thin slices ginger
1 tablespoon black tea-leaves

➤ PLACE EGGS in a medium pan and cover with cold water. Bring to the boil and simmer for 5 minutes.
1 Pour off water. Sharply tap the eggs all over with a spoon to crack shells.
2 Place remaining ingredients in the pan and bring to simmering point. Gently replace the eggs and simmer for 15 minutes, turning them over halfway through. Drain, peel under cold, running water.
3 Cut into quarters. Use as a cold entrée or a garnish for rice dishes.

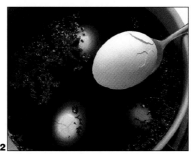

COOK'S FILE

Storage time: Eggs can be prepared to peeling stage 2 days ahead. Peel just before serving.
Hint: If you don't need half a dozen, 3 or 4 eggs can be prepared in the same quantity of cooking liquid.
Star anise is the shape of an irregular eight-pointed star, and has a flavour resembling that of liquorice. It is one of the essential components of Chinese five spice powder.

SCALLOP AND EGG FLOWER SOUP

Preparation time: 30 minutes
Cooking time: 45 minutes
Serves 4

300 g scallop meat
1 tablespoon dry sherry
¼ teaspoon ground white pepper
1 teaspoon grated ginger
2 tablespoons oil
3 spring onions, white part only, finely chopped
1 tablespoon cornflour
3 cups chicken stock
2 tablespoons soy sauce
⅓ cup canned straw mushrooms, cut in halves

⅓ cup frozen peas
1 egg, lightly beaten
4 spring onions, green part only, finely chopped
extra dry sherry, to taste
2 teaspoons soy sauce, extra

➤ COMBINE SCALLOPS, sherry, pepper and ginger. Leave 10 minutes in a cool place.
1 Heat the oil in a wok or heavy-based frying pan, swirling gently to coat base and side. Add the spring onion and cook briefly. Add scallops and their liquid and cook, turning, over a high heat until the scallops turn milky white. Transfer to a serving bowl.
2 Dissolve the cornflour in a little of the stock, add to the wok with the remaining stock. Add soy, bring to the

boil, stirring. Add straw mushrooms and peas and cook 2 minutes. Return the scallops to the wok, stir the soup continually.
3 Pour in the egg and cook only until it turns opaque. Stir the spring onion greens through and add a little more sherry and soy to taste.

COOK'S FILE

Storage time: Keep 1 day, covered, in the refrigerator Reheat gently over a low heat or the scallops will shrink and toughen.
Hint: Straw mushrooms have a 'meaty' texture and a savoury, rich fragrance. Drain and rinse before using.
Remaining canned mushrooms can be stored, covered with water, in the refrigerator. Use in another dish such as a stir-fry within 3 days.

Opposite: Marbled Soy Eggs (top),
Scallop and Egg Flower Soup (bottom).

NOODLES WITH PRAWNS AND PORK

Preparation time: 20 minutes
Cooking time: 10 minutes
Serves 4

10 large cooked prawns
200 g roast or Chinese
  barbecued pork (see recipe
  page 46)
500 g fresh, thick noodles (see
  Variation)
¼ cup peanut oil
2 teaspoons finely chopped
  garlic
1 tablespoon black bean sauce
1 tablespoon soy sauce
1 tablespoon commercial chilli
  and ginger sauce, optional
1 tablespoon white vinegar
¼ cup chicken stock
125 g fresh bean sprouts, tails
  removed
3 spring onions, finely sliced
¼ cup chopped fresh coriander,
  for garnish

➤ PEEL AND DEVEIN prawns. Cut the pork evenly into thin slices.

1 Cook the noodles in a large pan of rapidly boiling water until just tender; drain; set aside.

2 Heat oil in wok or heavy-based frying pan, swirling gently to coat base and side. Add the garlic and cook, stirring, until pale gold. Add the prawns and pork, stir for 1 minute. Add the noodles to the wok with the sauces, vinegar and stock. Stir-fry over a high heat until the mixture has heated through and the sauce has been absorbed.

3 Add the bean sprouts and the spring onion and cook 1 minute. Place in a serving dish; garnish with coriander.

COOK'S FILE

Storage time: This dish must be cooked just before serving.

Variation: Fresh, thick, egg and wheat noodles (hokkien mee) are ideal. If unavailable, you can substitute dried, thick spaghetti, cooking it first in plenty of boiling water until tender. If you enjoy a little 'fire' in your food, add a garnish of fresh chopped chillies or a splash of chilli oil at the end of cooking.

Hint: Chinese barbecued pork can be purchased ready-cooked from specialty Chinese stores.

ning water. Repeat procedure twice, using ½ teaspoon salt each time. Rinse prawns thoroughly the final time. Pat dry on absorbent paper.

2 Combine cornflour and egg white in a bowl, add prawns and marinate for 30 minutes in the refrigerator.

3 Wash and string the sugar snap peas; cut the capsicum into thin strips. Combine the reserved prawn liquid, oyster sauce, sherry, extra cornflour and sesame oil in a small bowl.

Heat the oil in a wok or deep, heavy-based frying pan. Gently lower prawns into moderately hot oil. Cook over medium-high heat for 1 to 2 minutes or until lightly golden. Carefully remove prawns from oil with tongs or a slotted spoon. Drain on absorbent paper. Keep warm.

4 Carefully pour all but 2 tablespoons of the oil into a heatproof dish. Add garlic and ginger. Stir-fry 30 seconds, add peas and capsicum, stir-fry over high heat 2 minutes. Add the combined sauce ingredients, cook, stirring, until sauce boils and thickens. Add prawns, stir to combine. Remove from heat. Serve immediately.

CRYSTAL PRAWNS

Preparation time: 15 minutes
  + 30 minutes marinating
Cooking time: 10 minutes
Serves 4

750 g medium green prawns
2 spring onions, roughly
  chopped
2 teaspoons salt
1 tablespoon cornflour
1 egg white, lightly beaten
125 g sugar snap peas or snow
  peas
1 small red capsicum
1 tablespoon oyster sauce
2 teaspoons dry sherry
1 teaspoon cornflour, extra
1 teaspoon sesame oil
oil for deep-frying
½ teaspoon crushed garlic
½ teaspoon finely grated ginger

➤ PEEL the prawns.
1 Devein. Place the shells, heads and the spring onion in a pan with water to cover; bring to the boil. Simmer,

uncovered, for 15 minutes. Strain into a bowl. Reserve ½ cup prawn liquid. Place the prawns in a glass bowl. Add 1 teaspoon of the salt and stir briskly for a minute. Rinse under cold, run-

Storage time: Cook this dish just before serving.

Hint: The salting process gives the prawns a crunchy texture that is much appreciated by lovers of Chinese food.

1

2

3

4

FRIED AND STEAMED SCALLOPS WITH GINGER

Preparation time: 5 minutes
Cooking time: 10 minutes
Serves 4 as an entrée

12 scallops on the shell
¼ teaspoon ground white
    pepper
2 tablespoons soy sauce
2 tablespoons dry sherry
2 tablespoons oil
8 cm piece ginger, peeled and
    shredded
spring onion, white part only,
    cut into long shreds

➤ SPRINKLE SCALLOPS with the pepper. Combine soy and sherry in a small bowl.

1 Heat the oil in a large, heavy-based pan until very hot. Carefully add several scallops face down and cook for 30 seconds to sear. Turn face up and arrange on a heatproof dish. Repeat with remaining scallops.

2 Sprinkle scallops with sherry-soy mixture and scatter a few shreds of ginger and spring onion over.

3 Fill a wok about one-third full with water and bring to a rolling boil. Place a steamer in the wok; place 6 scallops on it. Cover wok tightly and steam the scallops for 1 minute. Check for doneness; they may need about 30 seconds more. Remove and set aside to keep warm. Repeat steaming process with remaining scallops. Serve at once.

COOK'S FILE

Storage time: Cook this dish just before serving.

Variation: Scallops can be cooked by steaming only. This takes no more than 3 minutes (check after 2); they should be just cooked and still tender.

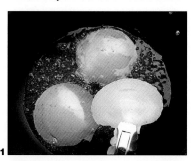

CRISPY FRIED CRAB

Preparation time: 30 minutes
    + overnight marinating
Cooking time: 15 minutes
Serves 4 as an entrée

1 x 1 kg live mud crab
1 egg, lightly beaten
1 red chilli, finely sliced
½ teaspoon crushed garlic
½ teaspoon salt
¼ teaspoon ground white pepper
oil for deep-frying

Seasoning Mix
4 tablespoons plain flour
4 tablespoons rice flour
3 teaspoons caster sugar
1 teaspoon ground white pepper

➤ PLACE CRAB in the freezer for 2 hours or until it is absolutely immobile.
1 Scrub crab clean of any mossy bits. Pull back apron from the underbelly and snap off. Twist off legs and claws. Pull the body apart and remove the feathery gills and internal organs. Using a sharp, heavy knife, chop the body into 4 pieces.
2 Crack the claws with a good hit with the back of the knife.
Beat the egg with the chilli, garlic, salt and pepper in a large bowl. Put the crab pieces in the mixture, cover and refrigerate overnight.

To make Seasoning Mix: Sift all seasoning ingredients together on a large plate. Dip all the crab segments in the seasoning and dust off excess.
3 Heat the oil in a wok or heavy-based frying pan until hot. Carefully cook the claws for 7 to 8 minutes, the body portions for 3 to 4 minutes, and the legs for 2 minutes. Drain all pieces on absorbent paper and serve.

COOK'S FILE

Storage time: Cook this dish just before serving.
Hint: Eat the crab with your fingers. You will need a mallet to crack the claws sufficiently to remove the flesh. This dish should be served on its own, without rice.

1

2

3

STEAMED FISH WITH GINGER

Preparation time: 45 minutes
Cooking time: 10 minutes
Serves 4

1 x 750 g snapper, cleaned and
    scaled
2 tablespoons finely grated
    ginger
2 teaspoons dry sherry
2 tablespoons soy sauce
2 tablespoons peanut oil
2 teaspoons sesame oil
2 spring onions, finely sliced
    diagonally

½ cup pine nuts, toasted
1 rasher bacon, diced and
    cooked until crisp, optional

➤ WASH SNAPPER, removing any
remaining loose scales; pat dry with
absorbent paper. Place fish on a large
heatproof dish; sprinkle with ginger,
sherry and soy. Leave 30 minutes in
the refrigerator.

1 Place a round cake-cooling rack in
a wok; balance the dish on it. Carefully
pour 6 to 8 cups of boiling water into
the wok. Cover the wok and steam the
fish over a rolling boil for 10 minutes.

2 Test for doneness by flaking a little
flesh from the thickest part of the fish
with a fork. It is ready when it flakes

easily and is milky white. Turn off
heat and keep dish covered.

3 Heat the oils in a small pan until
very hot. Carefully remove fish on its
dish from wok. Sprinkle the spring
onion over the fish, very carefully pour
on the hot oil. Garnish with nuts and
bacon, if used. Serve at once with stir-
fried vegetables and steamed rice.

COOK'S FILE

Storage time: Cook this dish just
before serving.

Hint: Even after the fishmonger has
scaled your fish, it can be left with a
number of scales, especially around the
head and tail. Rub your fingers up the fish,
removing scales as you come to them.

1

2

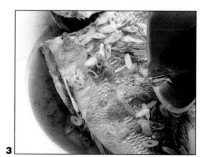

3

LEMON CHICKEN

Preparation time: 15 minutes
  + 30 minutes marinating
Cooking time: 10 minutes
Serves 4

500 g chicken breast fillets
1 egg white, lightly beaten
2 teaspoons cornflour
½ teaspoon salt
¼ teaspoon grated ginger
3 tablespoons oil

Lemon Sauce
2 teaspoons cornflour
2 tablespoons water

6 teaspoons caster sugar
2 tablespoons lemon juice
¾ cup chicken stock
2 teaspoons soy sauce
1 teaspoon dry sherry

➤ WASH CHICKEN under cold water. Pat dry with absorbent paper.
1 Cut the fillets on the diagonal into 1 cm wide strips. Combine the egg white, cornflour, salt and ginger in a bowl and add the chicken strips, mixing well. Marinate in the refrigerator for 30 minutes.
2 Heat the oil in a wok or heavy-based frying pan, swirling gently to coat base and side. Drain chicken from marinade, add to the pan and stir-fry over a moderately high heat until just cooked but not browned. Place chicken on a plate; keep warm while preparing the Sauce. Carefully pour excess oil from pan into a heatproof container.
3 **To make Lemon Sauce:** Mix cornflour with water to a smooth paste. Add to the wok with all the remaining sauce ingredients. Stir over high heat and boil for 1 minute. Add the chicken, stirring to coat it with the sauce. Transfer to a serving platter. Serve at once with steamed rice or noodles and stir-fried vegetables.

COOK'S FILE

Storage time: Cook this dish just before serving.

1

3

CLAY POT CHICKEN AND VEGETABLES

Preparation time: 20 minutes
 + 30 minutes marinating
Cooking time: 25 minutes
Serves 4

500 g chicken thigh fillets
1 tablespoon soy sauce
1 tablespoon dry sherry
6 dried Chinese mushrooms
2 small leeks
250 g orange sweet potato
2 tablespoons peanut oil
5 cm piece ginger, shredded
½ cup chicken stock,
    preferably homemade
1 teaspoon sesame oil
3 teaspoons cornflour

➤ WASH CHICKEN under cold water. Pat dry with absorbent paper. Cut into small pieces. Place in a dish with the soy sauce and the sherry, cover and marinate for 30 minutes in the refrigerator.

1 Soak mushrooms in hot water to cover for 30 minutes. Drain, squeeze to remove excess liquid. Remove stems and chop caps into shreds.
Wash leeks thoroughly to remove all grit; cut leeks and sweet potato into thin slices.

2 Drain the chicken, reserving the marinade. Heat half the oil in a wok or heavy-based frying pan, swirling it gently to coat base and side. Carefully add half the chicken pieces and stir-fry briefly until seared on all sides.
Transfer to a flameproof clay pot or casserole; stir-fry the remaining chicken and add to the clay pot.

3 Heat remaining oil in wok, add leek and ginger and stir-fry 1 minute. Add the mushrooms, the remaining marinade, the stock and sesame oil.

Transfer to the clay pot, add the sweet potato and cook, covered, on the top of the stove over a very low heat for about 20 minutes.
Dissolve cornflour with a little water and add to the pot. Cook, stirring, until the mixture boils and thickens.
Serve the chicken and vegetables at once with steamed brown or white rice or with noodles.

COOK'S FILE

Storage time: This is an example of a slow-cooked dish that can be cooked 1 to 2 days ahead. Store, covered, in the refrigerator. Bring to room temperature and reheat. Also suitable to freeze for about 1 month, but omit sweet potato. Steam or boil separately when dish is reheating; stir through.

1

2

3

HAINAN CHICKEN RICE

Preparation time: 30 minutes
Cooking time: 1 hour 30 minutes
Serves 4

1 x 1.5 kg chicken
1 sprig of celery leaves
few peppercorns
1 teaspoon salt
2 spring onions, roughly
  chopped
3 tablespoons peanut oil
1 tablespoon sesame oil
1 tablespoon finely grated ginger
2 teaspoons finely grated garlic
1 large onion, finely sliced
2 cups short-grain rice

Dipping Sauces
1 tablespoon finely grated
  ginger
2 tablespoons soy sauce
1 red chilli, chopped or
  1 teaspoon sambal oelek

Soup
1/2 cup finely shredded Chinese
  cabbage
2 tablespoons chopped fresh
  coriander

➤ WASH CHICKEN under cold
water. Place in a large pan with the
celery leaves, peppercorns, salt and
spring onion; cover with water. Cover
the pan, bring to the boil, simmer for
15 minutes. Turn off heat and leave,
covered, for 45 minutes.

1 Heat the oils in a pan with a well-
fitting lid. Add the ginger, garlic and
onion and cook until soft and golden.
Set aside 1 tablespoon of the oil to use
for a Dipping Sauce.

2 Add rice to pan and cook, stirring,
for 2 minutes. Add 3 cups of stock
from the pan in which the chicken was
cooked. Bring to the boil. Simmer until
holes appear in the rice.
Cover pan tightly and reduce heat to
very low. Cook for 15 minutes. Remove
the lid; fluff up the rice with a fork.

3 While rice is cooking, remove the
chicken from the pan, retaining the
stock for the Soup. Joint Western-style
or chop Chinese-style (see page 11).
Arrange pieces on a serving platter;
keep warm.

To make Dipping Sauces: Use
reserved tablespoon of cooking oils
and combine with grated ginger. For
the second sauce, combine soy sauce
and chilli.

To make Soup: The remaining stock
may be served alongside the rice dish
as a soup. Strain it, bring to the boil
and add the Chinese cabbage. Pour
into a bowl; sprinkle with coriander.
Serve chicken, rice and Dipping Sauces
with the bowl of hot chicken broth on
the side.

COOK'S FILE

Storage time: The chicken can be
cooked a day ahead and refrigerated.
Retain the stock in a separate, covered
container. Complete the dish just
before serving.

1

2

3

SMOKED FIVE SPICE CHICKEN

Preparation time: 30 minutes
  + overnight marinating
Cooking time: 35 minutes
Serves 6

1 x 1.7 kg chicken
¼ cup soy sauce
1 tablespoon finely grated
  ginger
2 medium pieces dried
  mandarin or tangerine peel
  (see page 11)
1 star anise
¼ teaspoon five spice powder
¼ cup soft brown sugar

➤ WASH CHICKEN in cold water. Pat dry with absorbent paper. Discard any large pieces of fat from inside the chicken.

1 Place the chicken in a large bowl with the soy and ginger. Cover and marinate for several hours or leave overnight in the refrigerator, turning occasionally.

2 Place a small rack in the base of a pan large enough to comfortably hold the chicken. Add water to this level. Place the chicken on the rack, bring water to the boil. Cover tightly, reduce heat and steam for 15 minutes. Turn off heat and allow to stand, covered, another 15 minutes. Transfer the chicken to a bowl.

3 Wash the pan and line with three or four large pieces of aluminium foil. Pound the dried peel and star anise in a mortar and pestle or crush with a rolling pin until pieces are the size of coarse breadcrumbs. Or, process in a food processor. Add five spice powder and sugar and spread over the foil.

4 Replace the rack in the pan and place the chicken on it. Place pan over a medium heat and, when spice mixture starts smoking, cover tightly. Reduce the heat to low; smoke the chicken for 20 minutes. Test for doneness by piercing the thigh with a skewer. The juices should run clear. Remove chicken from pan and joint it or chop it Chinese style (see page 11). It is important to remember that the heat produced in this final Step is very intense. When chicken is removed from pan, leave the pan on the stove to cool before handling it.

COOK'S FILE

Storage time: This dish can be cooked a day ahead.

Variation: If you wish to save on cooking time, try the same method using half chicken-breast fillets. Six fillets will take 7 minutes to steam; smoking will take 16 minutes, 8 each side. Overnight marinating is not necessary in this instance.

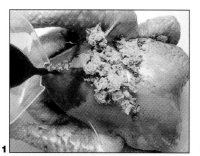
1

2

3

4

WHITE-COOKED CHICKEN WITH SPRING ONION SAUCE

Preparation time: 5 minutes
Cooking time: 1 hour + 1 hour chilling
Serves 6

1 x 1.8 kg chicken
3 slices ginger
1½ teaspoons salt
iced water (see Hint)

Spring Onion Sauce
2 tablespoons oil
3 spring onions, finely sliced
1 tablespoon soy sauce

➤ WASH CHICKEN under cold, running water.

1 Remove any pockets of fat from the carcass, remove and discard the tail. Place chicken in a large pan, fill with water to cover, add ginger and salt and bring to the boil. Cover, simmer for 20 minutes.

2 Turn off heat, keep the pan covered tightly. Leave for 35 minutes. Remove the chicken carefully from the pan, draining off any of the stock that has lodged inside.

Plunge the chicken into a large bowl full of iced water. This process stops the chicken cooking and tightens the skin, sealing in the juices.

3 Leave the cooled chicken in the bowl of iced water and chill in the refrigerator for 1 hour.

Just before serving, drain chicken from water and chop, Chinese style (see page 11).

To make Spring Onion Sauce: Heat the oil in a wok, add the spring onion and cook briefly just to heat through. Stir in the soy sauce. Serve the chicken with the Spring Onion Sauce poured over.

COOK'S FILE

Storage time: Chicken can be prepared 1 day ahead and stored in the refrigerator.

Hint: Use this recipe whenever cold, boiled chicken is called for. Because the chicken never boils and is chilled very rapidly, the juices are sealed in and the result is very succulent, moist and tender.

To achieve the result required, it is essential that the water into which the chicken is plunged is very well chilled. Add 2 or 3 trays of ice cubes to ensure that it is as cold as possible.

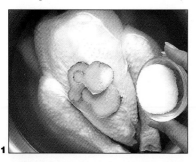

1

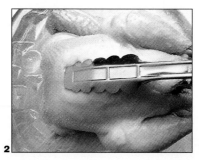

2

3

CRISP-SKINNED CHICKEN

Preparation time: 1 hour
Cooking time: 25 minutes
Serves 4

1 x 1.3 kg chicken
1 tablespoon honey
1 star anise
1 strip dried mandarin or
   tangerine peel
   (see page 11)
1 teaspoon salt
oil for deep-frying.
2 lemons, cut into wedges

Five Spice Salt
2 tablespoons sea salt
1 teaspoon white peppercorns

½ teaspoon five spice powder
½ teaspoon ground white
   pepper

➤ WASH CHICKEN in cold water. Place the chicken in a pan, cover with cold water, add honey, star anise, peel and salt and bring to the boil. Reduce heat to low and simmer 15 minutes. Turn off heat and leave chicken, covered, a further 15 minutes. Transfer chicken to a plate; cool.

1 Cut the chicken in half lengthways. Place on absorbent paper, uncovered, in the refrigerator for 20 minutes.

2 Heat the oil in a wok or deep, heavy-based pan. It is hot enough to use when a piece of bread turns brown in it in 30 seconds. Very gently lower in half the chicken, skin side down. Cook for 6 minutes, turn and cook

another 6 minutes, making sure all the skin comes in contact with the oil. Drain on absorbent paper. Repeat with second chicken half.

3 To make Five Spice Salt: Place salt and peppercorns in a small pan and dry-fry until the mixture smells fragrant and the salt is slightly browned. Crush with a mortar and pestle or wrap in aluminium foil and crush with a rolling pin. Mix with the five spice powder and white pepper and place in a tiny, shallow dish.

Joint the chicken (see page 11). Serve sprinkled with the Five Spice Salt and with lemon wedges.

COOK'S FILE

Storage time: Any leftover Five Spice Salt can be stored in a dry, airtight container for several months.

1

2

3

SPICED ROAST CHICKEN

Preparation time: 5 minutes
+ 1 hour marinating
Cooking time: 40 minutes
Serves 4

8 medium chicken drumsticks
1/3 cup soy sauce
2 teaspoons sesame oil
1 tablespoon oil
2 tablespoons dry sherry
1 teaspoon crushed garlic
1/2 teaspoon grated ginger

1 teaspoon five spice powder
1 tablespoon toasted sesame
    seeds, for garnish

➤ WASH CHICKEN in cold water.
Pat dry with absorbent paper.
1 Combine all ingredients in a dish,
cover and leave to marinate in the
refrigerator for at least 1 hour.
Preheat oven to moderate 180°C. Drain
chicken from marinade, place in a
baking dish and roast for 15 minutes.
2 Turn chicken pieces over and roast
a further 25 minutes.
3 Sprinkle with sesame seeds. Serve

hot with steamed rice or serve cold as
part of a buffet.

COOK'S FILE

Storage time: Can be cooked 1 day
ahead. Store, covered, in refrigerator.
Omit the sesame seeds, sprinkling
them on just before serving.
Hint: Chinese tea such as jasmine is
the appropriate drink to accompany
Chinese food; it is taken without sugar,
lemon or milk. Use fresh cold water
and bring to a rolling boil. Scald pot.
Add 1/2 to 1 teaspoon of tea leaves per
250 mL water. Cover; steep 3 minutes.

1

2

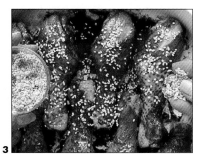
3

SALAD OF CHICKEN AND BEANS WITH PEANUT DRESSING

Preparation time: 15 minutes
+ 1 hour chilling
Cooking time: 20 minutes
Serves 4 as an entrée

3 chicken breast fillets
250 g green beans, topped and
    tailed

Satay Dressing
2 tablespoons peanut butter
1 tablespoon soy sauce
1 tablespoon white vinegar
1 tablespoon water

3 teaspoons caster sugar
2 teaspoons sesame oil

➤ WASH CHICKEN in cold water.
Pat dry with absorbent paper.
Place chicken breasts in a medium pan
with water to cover and bring slowly
to the boil over low heat. Cover, reduce
heat to a simmer and poach for 3
minutes. Remove pan from heat.
Leave, covered, for 20 minutes.
1 Slice the beans on the diagonal.
Cook briefly in a pan of boiling water
until crisp/tender. Drain in a colander,
place in a bowl of iced water to cool.
2 To make the Satay Dressing:
Warm the peanut butter slightly in a
small pan. Gradually mix in all the
remaining ingredients.

3 Drain the beans and pat dry in a
tea-towel. Arrange on serving platter.
Drain the breasts from the pan, slice
the meat across the grain.
Arrange the chicken over the beans.
Sprinkle with Satay Dressing. Chill for
1 hour before serving.

COOK'S FILE

Storage time: Cook chicken 1 day
ahead. Store, covered, in refrigerator.
Hint: Sesame oil has a strong flavour
and should be used in moderation. It
is often teamed with other milder oils,
such as peanut, in marinades and
sauces. A few drops can also be added
to the basic cooking oil in stir-fry
recipes. Store in the refrigerator after
opening to prevent rancidity.

1

2

3

*Opposite: Spiced Roast Chicken (top),
Salad of Chicken and Beans with Peanut Dressing (bottom).*

PEKING DUCK WITH MANDARIN PANCAKES

Preparation time: 1 hour + 4 hours standing time + 1 more hour for the pancakes
Cooking time: 1 hour
Serves 4 as a single course or 6 with other dishes

1 x 1.7 kg duck
3 litres boiling water
1 tablespoon honey
½ cup hot water
1 thin-skinned cucumber
12 spring onions
2 tablespoons hoisin sauce

Mandarin Pancakes
2½ cups plain flour
2 teaspoons caster sugar
1 cup boiling water
1 tablespoon sesame oil

➤ WASH DUCK, remove the neck and any large pieces of fat from inside the carcass.

1 Hold the duck over the sink and very carefully and slowly pour the boiling water over it, rotating the duck so the water scalds all the skin. You may need another kettle of boiling water at this stage.

2 Put the duck on a cake rack placed over a baking dish. Mix the honey and hot water together and brush two coats of this glaze over the duck, ensuring it is entirely covered.

Dry the duck, preferably hanging it up in a cool, airy place. Alternatively, you could use an electric fan on a cool setting, positioned a metre or so away. The skin is sufficiently dry when it is papery to the touch.

3 Remove seeds from cucumber and slice the flesh into matchsticks. Take an 8 cm section from each spring onion and make fine parallel cuts from the centre towards the end. Place in iced water; the spring onions will open into 'brushes'.

4 Preheat oven to moderately hot 210°C. Roast the duck on the rack over a baking pan for 30 minutes. Turn duck over carefully without tearing the skin, roast another 30 minutes. Remove from oven and let stand a minute or two. Place on a warm dish.

To make the Mandarin Pancakes: Place the flour and sugar in a medium bowl and pour over the boiling water. Stir the mixture a few times and leave until lukewarm.

Knead mixture on a lightly floured surface to make a smooth dough. Let stand for 30 minutes.

5 Take two level tablespoons of dough; roll each one into a ball. Roll out to circles of 8 cm diameter. Lightly brush one of the circles with sesame oil and place the other circle on top. Re-roll to make a thin pancake about 15 cm in diameter. Repeat with the remaining dough and oil to make about 10 'double' pancakes.

Heat a frying pan and cook the pancakes one at a time. When small bubbles appear on the surface, turn over and cook the second side, pressing the surface with a clean tea-towel. The pancake should puff up when done.

6 Remove to a plate. When cool enough to handle, peel the two pancakes apart. Stack them on a plate and cover at once to prevent them drying out.

To serve: Arrange the cucumber sticks and spring onion brushes on a serving plate. Place the hoisin sauce in a small dish. Place the pancakes and finely sliced duck on separate plates. Each guest helps themselves to a pancake, spreads a little sauce on it and adds a couple of pieces of cucumber, a spring onion brush and finally a piece of crisp duck skin. The pancake is then

folded over into a neat envelope shape for eating.

Follow the same procedure with the pancakes and duck meat when all the skin has been finished.

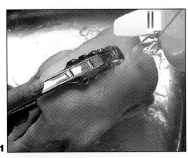

Storage time: The pancakes can be made a few hours ahead and kept covered in a cool place. Reheat briefly just before serving; you can either steam them in a colander lined with a clean tea-towel or wrap them securely in aluminium foil and place in a moderate oven for 2 minutes.

Hint: Traditionally, these pancakes should be paper-thin. Once you have mastered the technique of making them, use one level tablespoon of the dough for each and proceed as before.

4

5

6

DUCK IN ORANGE SAUCE

Preparation time: 20 minutes
Cooking time: 2 hours
Serves 4

1 x 1.6 kg duck
3 slices ginger
1/4 teaspoon five spice powder
1/4 teaspoon ground white
    pepper
2 tablespoons dry sherry
oil for deep-frying

Orange Sauce
1/2 cup orange juice
6 teaspoons lemon juice
1 tablespoon finely grated
    orange rind
1 tablespoon soy sauce
1 tablespoon soft brown sugar
2 teaspoons cornflour

➤ WASH DUCK in cold water. Pat dry with absorbent paper.

1 Remove and discard the tail and large pieces of fat from the inside of the duck carcass. Using scissors, cut the duck in half and remove the neck and first two wing joints. Cut the duck halves in half again. Place neck and wing joints in a pot, cover with water and simmer for 30 minutes to make stock. Strain into a bowl.

2 Place quartered duck in a pan with water to almost cover. Add ginger, five spice powder, pepper and sherry. Bring to the boil, reduce to a simmer and cook, covered, for 1 1/2 hours. Add the reserved stock.

3 Remove the duck quarters from the cooking liquid and leave to cool. Continue cooking the liquid until reduced to about 3/4 cup stock.

To make Sauce: Strain the stock and combine with the orange and lemon juice, rind, soy and sugar. Simmer for 5 minutes. Dissolve the cornflour in a little water and add to the pan. Stir until thickened; simmer 3 minutes.

4 Heat oil in a wok or deep, heavy-based pan and deep-fry duck pieces, two at a time, until skin is crisp, about 3 minutes. Drain on absorbent paper. When cool enough to handle, gently remove the flesh from each quarter and slice into three or four pieces. Arrange the duck pieces on a serving platter and pour Orange Sauce over.

COOK'S FILE

Storage time: Duck can be cooked up to the frying stage 1 day ahead. Fry the duck and prepare the sauce just before serving.

Hint: When deep-frying in a wok, it is vital that the wok is placed in a stable position. Make sure that the handle is not protruding where it can easily be knocked. When cooking with hot oil, do not leave unattended at any time.

1

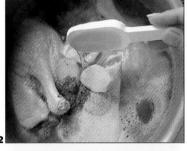
2

3

4

STIR-FRIED BEEF AND SNOW PEAS

Preparation time: 10 minutes
Cooking time: 5 minutes
Serves 4

400 g rump steak, finely sliced
2 tablespoons soy sauce
1/2 teaspoon grated ginger
2 tablespoons peanut oil
200 g snow peas, topped and tailed

1 1/2 teaspoons cornflour
1/2 cup beef stock
1 teaspoon soy sauce, extra
1/4 teaspoon sesame oil

➤ PLACE MEAT in a dish. Mix soy and ginger and stir through meat to coat.

1 Heat the oil in a wok or a heavy-based frying pan, swirling gently to coat base and side. Add the beef and snow peas and stir-fry over a high heat for 2 minutes, or until the meat changes colour.

2 Dissolve the cornflour in a little of the stock. Add to the wok with the remaining stock, extra soy and the sesame oil.

3 Stir until sauce boils and thickens. Serve with steamed rice.

COOK'S FILE

Storage time: Cook this dish just before serving.

Hint: If time allows, place meat in the freezer for 30 minutes before slicing. This will firm it and make slicing it finely much easier.

1

2

3

BEEF IN BLACK BEAN SAUCE

Preparation time: 10 minutes
Cooking time: 10 minutes
Serves 4

2 tablespoons salted black beans
1 medium onion
1 small red capsicum
1 small green capsicum
2 teaspoons cornflour
½ cup beef stock
2 teaspoons soy sauce
1 teaspoon sugar
2 tablespoons oil
1 teaspoon finely crushed garlic
¼ teaspoon ground black
   pepper
400 g rump or fillet steak,
   finely sliced

➤ RINSE BLACK BEANS in several changes of water.

1 Drain and mash black beans. Cut the onion into wedges. Halve the capsicum, discard seeds and cut into small pieces. Dissolve cornflour in stock, add soy and sugar.

2 Heat 1 tablespoon of the oil in a wok or heavy-based frying pan, swirling gently to coat base and side. Add garlic, pepper, onion and capsicum and stir-fry over high heat for 1 minute; remove to a bowl.

3 Add remaining tablespoon of oil, swirling gently to coat base and side of wok. Add beef and stir-fry over a high heat for 2 minutes, until it changes colour.

Add black beans, cornflour mixture and vegetables. Stir until sauce boils and thickens. Serve with steamed rice.

COOK'S FILE

Storage time: Cook this dish just before serving.

1

3

BEEF WITH MANDARIN

Preparation time: 25 minutes
Cooking time: 5 minutes
Serves 4

350 g boned rib eye, finely sliced
2 teaspoons soy sauce
2 teaspoons dry sherry
1 teaspoon chopped ginger
1 teaspoon sesame oil
1 tablespoon peanut oil
1/4 teaspoon ground white
   pepper
2 teaspoons finely chopped
   dried mandarin or tangerine
   rind (see page 11)
2 teaspoons soy sauce, extra
1 1/2 teaspoons caster sugar
1 1/2 teaspoons cornflour
1/3 cup beef stock

➤ PLACE MEAT in a bowl.
1 Mix soy, sherry, ginger and sesame oil together, stir through meat to coat. Let stand 15 minutes.
Heat the oil in a wok or heavy-based frying pan, swirling gently to coat base and side. Add beef and stir-fry over high heat for 2 minutes, until meat changes colour.
2 Add the pepper, rind, extra soy and sugar. Stir-fry briefly.
3 Dissolve the cornflour in a little of the stock, add remaining stock. Add cornflour mixture to the wok. Stir until the sauce boils and thickens. Serve with rice or steamed breads.

COOK'S FILE

Storage time: Cook just before serving.
Variation: Fry 1 dried chilli in the hot oil before adding the beef; discard the chilli before stir-frying.
The thickened sauce is optional. You can dry-fry the marinated beef dish; serve with fine noodles instead of rice.

Hint: The more expensive, tender cuts of beef such as rib eye or rump are best for stir-frying. However, a cheaper cut such as round or blade can be used but should be tenderised in a marinade after it has been finely sliced. Dissolve 1/2 teaspoon bicarbonate of soda in 2 tablespoons warm water. Place beef in a dish, pour over marinade and knead it through meat. Cover and refrigerate for 2 hours. Bring to room temperature; continue with recipe.

1

2

3

STIR-FRIED BEEF AND VEGETABLES

Preparation time: 15 minutes
Cooking time: 5 minutes
Serves 4

1½ teaspoons cornflour
½ cup beef stock
2 tablespoons oyster sauce
1 teaspoon finely crushed garlic
1 teaspoon caster sugar

2 tablespoons peanut oil
350 g rump steak, finely sliced
250 g beans, topped and tailed,
  cut in 5 cm lengths
1 small red capsicum, sliced
½ cup fresh bean sprouts, tails
  removed, optional

➤ DISSOLVE THE CORNFLOUR in
a little of the stock. Add remaining
stock, oyster sauce, garlic and sugar.
Set mixture aside.
1 Heat oil in a wok or heavy-based

frying pan, swirling gently to coat
base and side. Add beef, stir-fry over
high heat for 2 minutes, or until it
changes colour.
2 Add beans and capsicum and stir-
fry another minute.
3 Add the cornflour mixture and cook
until the sauce boils and thickens. Stir
in bean sprouts. Serve with boiled rice.

COOK'S FILE

Storage time: Cook this dish just
before serving.

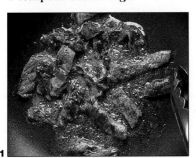

CHINESE BARBECUED PORK

Preparation time: 40 minutes
+ 30 minutes marinating
Cooking time: 35 minutes
Serves 6

750 g pork neck or fillet
1/4 cup tomato sauce
1 tablespoon hoisin sauce
2 tablespoons honey
1 tablespoon malt extract or
   molasses
1 tablespoon chopped garlic
2 tablespoons caster sugar
1 teaspoon five spice powder
2 teaspoons cornflour
1 tablespoon water

➤ PLACE MEAT in freezer for about 30 minutes to firm.

1 Combine the tomato sauce, hoisin sauce, honey, malt extract, garlic, sugar and five spice powder in a small pan. Dissolve the cornflour in the water and add to the mixture. Bring to the boil, reduce to a simmer and stir for 2 minutes. Cool.

If using pork neck, cut lengthways in half. Pork fillets will not need to be cut. Place meat in the sauce, turning to coat; marinate for at least 30 minutes.

2 Preheat oven to moderately hot 210°C. Drain pork from marinade and place on a wire rack set over a baking tray half-filled with hot water. Cook the pork for 15 minutes.

3 Reduce heat and cook pork a further 15 minutes, basting occasionally with the remaining marinade. Remove from oven and let stand for 5 minutes before slicing and serving.

COOK'S FILE

Storage time: Cook this dish just before serving.

Hint: Long strips of barbecued pork are seen hanging alongside roast pork and ducks in the windows of Chinese food shops. Chinese roasting involves hanging the pieces of meat on hooks in large ovens. If you have a local supplier, use this ready-cooked pork for a quick and easy meal with stir-fried vegetables and rice.

Chinese five spice powder is a blend of Chinese brown peppercorns, cinnamon bark, cloves, fennel and star anise. Keep stored in an airtight container.

CHILLI SPARE RIBS

Preparation time: 20 minutes
Cooking time: 1 hour
Serves 4

750 g pork spare ribs
1 tablespoon peanut oil
2 teaspoons finely chopped
   garlic
1/4 cup dry sherry
1 tablespoon chilli bean paste
   or sambal oelek

2 cups water
2 teaspoons hoisin sauce
3 teaspoons caster sugar
1 tablespoon soy sauce,
   preferably dark

➤ PLACE PORK in a large pan with water to cover. Bring to the boil, reduce heat, simmer for 5 minutes, drain and set pork aside.

1 In a wok or deep, heavy-based pan, place all remaining ingredients and the pork ribs. Cover, simmer 45 minutes. Drain, reserving 1 cup of liquid.

Heat a clean wok or heavy-based frying pan and sear the pork pieces to brown them.

2 Add the reserved cooking liquid and cook over a medium heat until it forms a glazed coating for the pork.

3 Chop the pork pieces into 3 cm pieces and serve with the sauce poured over them.

COOK'S FILE

Storage time: This dish can be cooked 1 day ahead and reheated. Store, covered, in the refrigerator.

Opposite: Chinese Barbecued Pork (top),
Chilli Spare Ribs (bottom).

PORK CHOW MEIN

Preparation time: 30 minutes
Cooking time: 25 minutes
Serves 4

250 g fresh, thin egg noodles
   or Italian vermicelli
1 medium onion
1 medium carrot
4 spring onions
1 small green capsicum
1 small red capsicum
5 tablespoons oil
1 teaspoon finely chopped garlic
2 teaspoons finely chopped
   ginger
4 tablespoons chopped ham fat
1 cup cubed cooked pork or ham
6 teaspoons Chinese char sui
   sauce (see Variation)
½ cup bean sprouts, tails
   removed
3 teaspoons cornflour
1¼ cups chicken stock

➤ PLACE NOODLES in a large pan of boiling water and cook until just tender.

1 Drain noodles in a colander. Spread out on a clean tea-towel to dry.
Cut onion into quarters or eighths and separate the layers. Cut carrot into thin strips.

2 Cut spring onions into 5 cm lengths and the capsicum into 2.5 cm squares.

3 Heat 1 tablespoon of the oil in a heavy-based pan. Add half the noodles and cook over a moderate heat for 5 minutes or until a golden, crisp 'cake' has formed. Turn noodle cake over and cook a further 5 minutes, adding another tablespoon of oil by drizzling it down the side of the pan. Remove noodles to a plate and keep warm. Repeat this procedure with the remaining noodles.

4 Heat remaining oil in a wok and cook the garlic and ginger until light golden. Add the onion, carrot, spring onion and capsicum and toss over a high heat for 3 minutes.

5 Add the ham fat, pork and char sui sauce and cook a further minute. Add bean sprouts and toss for a few seconds.

6 Dissolve the cornflour in a little of the stock. Add with remaining stock to wok. Stir until the liquid boils and thickens.
Place noodle cakes on a serving platter and use a knife to break them up. Pour pork mixture over. Serve immediately.

COOK'S FILE

Storage time: Cook this dish just before serving.

Variation: If bottled char sui sauce is not available, substitute 1 tablespoon hoisin sauce. This is a dark, reddish brown sauce made from ground fermented soybeans, wheat flour, garlic, sugar and red rice. This last is not the true red rice of Sri Lanka but white rice that has been made red with food colouring.
Hoisin is the traditional accompaniment to Peking roast duck and also goes well with pork dishes. Meat glazed with hoisin during cooking take on a rather rosy appearance.

Hint: Chopped ham fat is available from your butcher.
To remove fat from the surface of homemade stock, it is easiest first to cool and refrigerate the liquid. The fat will rise to the surface and harden. Then, this solid disk of fat is simply lifted off and discarded.
Hot stock can be skimmed with a ladle, but as this method won't be sufficient to remove all the fat, it will be necessary to lightly float a paper towel on the surface to remove the last traces of grease.

CRISP ROAST PORK

Preparation time: 30 minutes
Cooking time: 1 hour
Serves 4

2 teaspoons salt
½ teaspoon ground white
 pepper
½ teaspoon five spice powder
1.5 kg belly of pork
1 tablespoon hoisin sauce

➤ COMBINE salt, pepper and five spice powder.

1 Prick the pork skin all over with a skewer. Rub 1½ teaspoons of the salt mixture into the skin.

2 Turn the piece of pork over and make shallow cuts at about 3 cm intervals across the width of the belly. Rub in the remaining salt mixture and the hoisin sauce.

3 Preheat oven to moderately hot 210°C. Place the pork, skin side up, on a wire rack set over a baking tray half-filled with hot water. Cook pork for 15 minutes. Reduce temperature to moderate 180°C and cook 40 minutes. Remove from oven. If the skin has not turned to crackling, place pork under a hot grill for about 2 minutes; watch carefully to prevent burning.

4 Leave the pork for 5 minutes. Turn skin side down. Chop through the 3 cm wide strips; cut each strip in half. Serve hot with rice.

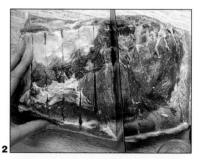

50

FRIED RICE

Preparation time: 15 minutes
Cooking time: 10 minutes
Serves 4

2 eggs, lightly beaten
1 medium onion
4 spring onions
250 g ham in the piece
2 tablespoons peanut oil
2 teaspoons lard,
   optional
4 cups cold, cooked rice
¼ cup frozen peas
2 tablespoons soy sauce
250 g cooked small prawns,
   peeled

➤ SEASON THE EGGS with salt
and pepper.
1 Peel onion and cut into wedges
about 1.5 cm wide. Cut spring onions
into short lengths on the diagonal. Cut
the ham into very thin strips.
Heat 1 tablespoon oil in a wok or large
frying pan and add the eggs, pulling
the set egg towards the centre and
tilting the pan to let the unset egg run
to the edges.
2 When almost set, break up into
large pieces, to resemble scrambled
eggs. Transfer to a plate and set aside.
3 Heat the remaining oil and lard in
the wok, swirling to coat base and
side. Add the onion and stir-fry over
high heat until it starts to turn
transparent. Add the ham, stir-fry for

1 minute. Add rice and peas, stir-fry
for 3 minutes until the rice is heated
through. Add eggs, soy, spring onion
and prawns. Heat through; serve.

COOK'S FILE

Storage time: Cook the rice for
frying 1 day ahead. Store, covered, in
the refrigerator.
Variation: This dish is traditionally
served as a snack or course in its own
right rather than as an accompaniment
to other dishes. The ingredients can be
varied to suit your taste; use barbecued pork, lap cheong, (Chinese
sausage) or bacon instead of ham.
Hint: Lard is rendered, strained pork
fat which is used in both meat and
vegetable recipes.

1

2

3

CHINESE-STYLE BROCCOLI SALAD

Preparation time: 15 minutes
Cooking time: 5 minutes
Serves 4

750 g broccoli
1 small red capsicum
iced water
2 tablespoons peanut oil
2 teaspoons sesame oil
2 teaspoons finely minced ginger
2 tablespoons soy sauce
1 tablespoon water
1 tablespoon sesame seeds,
   toasted

2 spring onions, green part
   only, finely sliced

➤ CUT BROCCOLI into medium
florets.
1 Peel tough skin from stems. Cut
tender part into small pieces. Slice the
capsicum very thinly and set aside.
2 Bring a pan of water to a rolling
boil, add the broccoli and cook for 2 to
3 minutes until crisp/tender. Strain off
water and plunge broccoli into iced
water to stop the cooking process and
set the bright colour. Drain in a
colander. Pat dry on absorbent paper.
Place in a serving bowl with capsicum.
3 Combine the oils, ginger, soy and
water and pour over the salad. Cover,

refrigerate. Sprinkle with sesame seeds
and spring onion just before serving.

C O O K ' S   F I L E

Storage time: Prepare salad and
refrigerate 2 hours in advance. Add
sesame seeds just before serving.
Hint: To toast sesame seeds, place
them in a small, dry pan over medium
heat until golden. Stir frequently to
make sure that they do not burn.
The method of plunging the vegetable
into iced water to set its colour and
arrest the cooking process is a useful
one for other green vegetables such as
Chinese leaf vegetables, beans and
snow peas. It will greatly enhance the
look of the finished dish.

STIR-FRIED MIXED VEGETABLES

Preparation time: 5 minutes
Cooking time: 4 minutes
Serves 4

1 medium carrot
1 medium red capsicum
125 g green beans
1 tablespoon oil
1 teaspoon finely chopped garlic
200 g straw mushrooms
1½ teaspoons cornflour
⅓ cup chicken stock

1 teaspoon sesame oil
1 teaspoon caster sugar
2 teaspoons soy sauce

➤ SLICE CARROT finely.
1 Seed capsicum and cut into 4 cm
pieces. Top and tail the beans and cut
them in half.
2 Heat the oil in a wok or heavy-
based frying pan, swirling gently to
coat base and side.
Add the carrot and stir-fry over a high
heat for 30 seconds. Stir in the garlic;
add the remaining vegetables and stir-
fry them over high heat for 2 minutes;
they must still be very crisp and firm.

3 Dissolve cornflour in a little of the
stock. Mix with remaining stock,
sesame oil, sugar and soy. Add to
wok, stir until sauce thickens. Serve
immediately with steamed rice.

C O O K ' S   F I L E

Storage time: Cook this dish just
before serving.
Variation: This recipe can be easily
varied to include many different
vegetables. Try using a combination
of Chinese greens, cutting them into
short lengths. They will need the
briefest cooking time to prevent them
turning limp.

Opposite: Chinese-style Broccoli Salad (top),
Stir-fried Mixed Vegetables (bottom).

CHINESE VEGETABLES

Preparation time: 10 minutes
Cooking time: 5 minutes
Serves 4

1 bunch Chinese green
  vegetables such as choy sum
2 teaspoons peanut oil
½ teaspoon finely chopped
  garlic

1 tablespoon oyster sauce
½ teaspoon caster sugar
2 tablespoons water
1 teaspoon sesame oil

➤ BRING A LARGE PAN of water
to the boil.
1 Wash Chinese greens. Remove any
tough leaves, trim stems. Chop greens
into three equal portions.
2 Add the greens to the pan of boiling
water. Cook 1 to 2 minutes, or until

just tender but still crisp. Using tongs,
remove greens from the pan. Place on
a heated serving platter.
3 Heat the oil in a small pan, add the
garlic, cook briefly. Add oyster sauce,
sugar, water and sesame oil, bring to
the boil. Pour over greens; toss to coat
with sauce. Serve immediately.

COOK'S FILE

Storage time: Cook this dish just
before serving.

SWEET GARLIC EGGPLANT

Preparation time: 5 minutes
Cooking time: 15 minutes
Serves 4

3 medium eggplant
7 tablespoons oil
1½ teaspoons finely chopped
　garlic
6 teaspoons caster sugar
6 teaspoons soy sauce,
　preferably dark
6 teaspoons cider vinegar
1 tablespoon dry sherry

➤ CUT THE EGGPLANT in half lengthways, then into 3 cm wide wedges.

1 Cut wedges into pieces about 3 cm long.

2 Heat a wok or heavy-based frying pan, add 3 tablespoons of the oil, swirling gently to coat base and side. Add half the eggplant pieces and stir-fry over high heat for 5 minutes, or until browned and oil is all absorbed. Transfer to a plate; repeat cooking procedure with another 3 tablespoons oil and the remaining eggplant.

3 Heat the remaining oil in the wok, swirling gently to coat base and side. Add garlic and cook slowly until just golden. Add sugar, soy, vinegar and sherry. Bring to the boil, stirring.

Add eggplant and simmer 3 minutes to allow it to absorb the sauce. Turn onto a serving platter. Serve with white rice.

COOK'S FILE

Storage time: This dish can also be cooked 2 days ahead and served at room temperature.

Variation: Vary the amount of sugar to suit your taste.

HONEY-BRAISED VEGETABLES WITH BEAN CURD

Preparation time: 30 minutes
Cooking time: 15 minutes
Serves 6

8 dried Chinese mushrooms
20 dried lily buds (optional)
2 tablespoons peanut oil
3 thin slices ginger
250 g white sweet potato,
   halved and sliced
2 tablespoons soy sauce
1 tablespoon honey
2 teaspoons sesame oil
45 g fried bean curd, cut into
   1 cm strips
2 teaspoons cornflour
4 spring onions cut into
   4 cm lengths
1 x 410 g can baby corn
1 x 230 g canned water
   chestnuts, drained

➤ SOAK MUSHROOMS in hot water to cover for 30 minutes.

1 Drain, reserving ¾ cup liquid. Squeeze mushrooms to remove excess liquid. Remove stems. Slice the mushrooms thinly. Slice ginger thinly. Soak the lily buds separately, if using, in warm water for 30 minutes; drain.

2 Heat the oil in a wok or heavy-based frying pan, swirling gently to coat base and side. Add ginger and stir-fry over medium heat for 1 minute. Add the mushrooms and lily buds and stir-fry for 30 seconds. Add sweet potato with the soy, honey, sesame oil, mushroom liquid and fried bean curd. Simmer, uncovered, 15 minutes.

3 Dissolve cornflour in a little water, add to pan. Stir until liquid thickens. Add the spring onions, corn and water chestnuts; simmer 1 minute.

COOK'S FILE

Storage time: Cook this dish just before serving.
Variation: Soft bean curd can be used in place of fried. In this case, cut it into 2 cm cubes, slide them carefully into the wok after the spring onions, corn and water chestnuts. and heat through gently. If too hot, curd will break up.

1

2

3

ALMOND JELLY

Preparation time: 5 minutes
+ 1 hour chilling
Cooking time: 5 minutes
Serves 4 to 6

2 cups cold water
⅓ cup caster sugar
2 teaspoons agar agar
1 x 150 mL can evaporated milk
½ teaspoon almond essence

3 fresh mandarins, peeled and
segmented or 300 g fresh
cherries, pitted and chilled

➤ PLACE WATER and sugar in a
small pan.
1 Sprinkle the agar agar powder over.
Bring to the boil, simmer 1 minute.
Add the evaporated milk and essence.
2 Pour into a shallow 18 x 27 cm pan
to set. Chill for at least an hour.
3 Cut the jelly into diamonds shapes,
serve with fruit.

COOK'S FILE

Storage time: Cook 1 day ahead.
Variation: Agar agar is similar to
gelatine but does not need
refrigeration to help it set. If it is
unavailable, use 3 teaspoons of
gelatine sprinkled over ½ cup cold
water to soften. Stir into the water and
sugar mixture, bring to the boil,
remove from heat. There is no need to
simmer. Proceed with the method;
refrigeration time will be 5 hours.

EGG TARTS

Preparation time: 10 minutes
Cooking time: 15 to 18 minutes
Makes 18

Outer Dough
1⅓ cups plain flour
2 tablespoons icing sugar
⅓ cup water
2 tablespoons oil

Inner Dough
1 cup plain flour
100 g lard, chopped

Custard
⅓ cup water
¼ cup caster sugar
2 eggs, lightly beaten

➤ PREHEAT OVEN to moderately hot 210°C. Brush 2 x 12 cup shallow patty tins with melted butter or oil.

1 To make the Outer Dough: Sift combined flour and sugar in a medium bowl. Make a well in the centre. Pour in the combined water and oil. Stir quickly, then knead to form a soft dough. (If flour is very dry, a little extra water may be necessary.) Cover and set aside; leave for 15 minutes.

To make Inner Dough: Sift flour into a medium bowl. Using fingertips, rub lard into flour until mixture resembles coarse breadcrumbs. Knead mixture to form a very short-textured pastry. Cover and set aside; leave for 15 minutes.

Take the Outer Dough. On a lightly floured surface, roll into a rectangle about 20 x 10 cm.

Roll the Inner Dough on a lightly floured surface into a smaller rectangle, one third the size of the other. Place the Inner Dough on the centre of the Outer Dough. Fold over edges to thoroughly enclose; pinch the ends together to seal.

2 Roll dough out on a lightly floured surface into a long rectangle, about half as thick as it was previously. Take the left-hand edge and bring it towards the centre. Repeat with the right-hand edge. Wrap the dough in plastic wrap and leave in a cool place for 30 minutes.

3 To make the Custard: Place water and sugar in a pan and bring to the boil. Simmer, uncovered, until the sugar has dissolved. Cool the mixture for 5 minutes.

Whisk the sugar syrup into the eggs until just combined. Strain into a jug.

4 Turn the pastry so that the fold is on the left-hand side. Working on a lightly floured surface, roll pastry out to a rectangle of about 3 mm thickness. Cut out rounds using a 7 cm fluted cutter. Carefully place pastry rounds into prepared patty tins.

5 Fill each pastry case two-thirds full with the egg custard mixture. Cook for 15 to 18 minutes. Do not overcook; the filling should be just set.

6 Leave egg tarts for 3 minutes before removing them from tin. Slip a flat-bladed knife down the side of each tart to help lift it out. Cool on a wire rack. Serve warm.

COOK'S FILE

Storage time: Egg tarts can also be eaten cold. Cook 2 days ahead. Store in an airtight container.

Hint: The pastry in this recipe has a delicious, distinctive taste and texture. However, if you prefer not to make your own pastry, or are short on time, ready-rolled frozen shortcrust pastry can be used. A good (though not authentic), result can be achieved. You will need to use three sheets of pastry for this quantity of tarts. Thaw to room temperature before using.

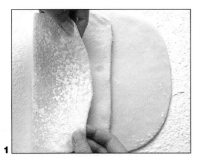

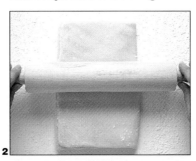

4

5

6

SOUTH EAST ASIAN

BEEF SOUP WITH RICE NOODLES

Preparation time: 30 minutes
Cooking time: 1 hour + 1 hour
    marinating
Serves 4

350 g fillet steak
2 teaspoons soy sauce
¼ cup coconut milk
1 tablespoon crunchy peanut
    butter
1 tablespoon soft brown or
    palm sugar
2 teaspoons sambal oelek
    or 1 small red chilli,
    finely chopped
1 teaspoon oil
125 g rice vermicelli
1 small, thin-skinned cucumber
6 cups beef stock
2 tablespoons soft brown sugar,
    extra
2 tablespoons fish sauce
1 cup fresh bean sprouts, tails
    removed
2 lettuce leaves, cut in small
    pieces
6 tablespoons finely chopped
    fresh mint leaves
½ cup roasted peanuts, finely
    chopped

➤ TRIM MEAT of any fat and sinew. Slice meat across the grain evenly into thin slices.
1 Combine meat with soy sauce, coconut milk, peanut butter, sugar and sambal oelek. Leave in refrigerator, covered, for 1 hour.
2 Heat oil in pan. Cook meat in small batches over a high heat for 3 minutes, until browned. Remove from heat, cover. Soak rice vermicelli in hot water for 10 minutes. Drain.
3 Cut cucumber in quarters lengthways and then into thin slices. Heat stock to boiling point. When boiling, add extra sugar and fish sauce.
Place about 1 tablespoon cucumber slices in each serving bowl; divide bean sprouts, pieces of lettuce and mint leaves evenly between bowls.
Place some vermicelli and a ladle of stock in each bowl, top with slices of cooked beef. Sprinkle with peanuts and serve immediately.

COOK'S FILE

Storage time: Cook just before serving.
Hint: Make your own sambal oelek by placing 20 finely chopped red chillies (handle with care, keeping your hands away from your eyes) and 2 teaspoons sea salt in a food processor; process to combine. Place in sterilised, airtight jar; store in refrigerator for up to 1 month.

3

SEAFOOD LAKSA

Preparation time: 45 minutes
Cooking time: 35 minutes
Serves 4

1 kg large green prawns
5 tablespoons oil
1 litre water
6 large red chillies, seeded
1 large onion, roughly chopped
2 cloves garlic, peeled
3 slices ginger or galangal
1 teaspoon turmeric
1 tablespoon ground coriander
6 macadamia nuts
1 teaspoon shrimp paste
2 stalks lemon grass, thick base
    only
1 x 400 mL can coconut milk
3 teaspoons salt
3 teaspoons soft brown or palm
    sugar
500 g fresh, thick rice noodles
    or 125 g dried rice noodles
    or vermicelli
2 small, thin-skinned cucumbers
250 g fresh bean sprouts, tails
    removed
⅓ cup chopped fresh mint or
    Vietnamese mint sprigs

➤ PEEL AND DEVEIN prawns, keeping the end section and tail intact. Reserve heads and shells.

1 Heat 2 tablespoons of the oil in a large pan, add the prawn heads and shells. Stir and toss them about until they turn bright orange; add the water. Bring to the boil, reduce to a simmer. Cook for 15 minutes, strain stock into a clean pan, discard shells.

2 Place chillies, onion, garlic, ginger, turmeric, coriander and macadamia nuts in a food processor bowl or blender. Process until smooth, adding a little water, if necessary.

Heat remaining 3 tablespoons of oil in a wok and add the mixture from the processor. Add shrimp paste and stir well to combine. Bruise lemon grass with a cleaver or heavy, flat-bladed knife and add to the pan. Cook for 3 to 4 minutes, stirring frequently.

Add the reserved stock and simmer for 10 minutes. Add the coconut milk, the salt and the sugar; simmer, uncovered, for 5 minutes. Add the prawns, cook, uncovered, 2 minutes or until just pink. Remove prawns using slotted spoon; set aside.

3 Meanwhile, bring a pan of water to the boil and add noodles. If using fresh noodles, boil 1 minute. Dried will take barely 2 minutes for the thin and about 5 minutes for the thick. Drain. Cut cucumber into thin, 5 cm lengths. Place noodles in a large soup tureen, top with the cucumber, bean sprouts

and prawns. Bring the soup back to boiling point; pour it over the noodles. Each diner sprinkles on mint to taste.

COOK'S FILE

Storage time: The prawns and the broth can be prepared a few hours ahead; however, in this instance, do not cook prawns in the broth until just before serving time or they will be overcooked and tough.

Variation: Thick-skinned cucumbers can be used in place of thin. Peel before use.

Hint: Vietnamese mint has a very distinctive, peppery, hot taste, quite unlike that of conventional mint. For this recipe, the flavour of Vietnamese mint is the authentic one required. The pungent shrimp paste is also essential. Because of its intensity, it must always be used sparingly.

1

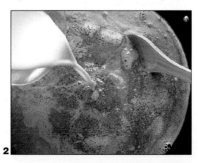

2

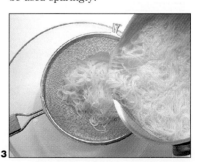

3

HOT AND SOUR THAI PRAWN SOUP

Preparation time: 10 minutes
Cooking time: 20 minutes
Serves 4

400 g medium green prawns
1 tablespoon oil
6 cups water
1 teaspoon roughly chopped
  garlic
¾ teaspoon salt
3 dried or fresh Kaffir lime
  leaves
4 red chillies
1 stalk lemon grass, thick base
  only, roughly chopped
1 tablespoon roughly chopped
  fresh coriander
2 spring onions, finely sliced
1 red chilli, extra, finely sliced
6 teaspoons fish sauce
2 tablespoons lime juice

➤ PEEL AND DEVEIN prawns. Reserve heads and shells. Heat the oil in a pan and, when very hot, add the prawn shells and heads. Cook over high heat until they turn pink.

1 Add the water, garlic, salt, lime leaves, chillies and lemon grass. Bring to the boil, reduce to a simmer and cook, uncovered, for 15 minutes.

2 Strain the stock into a clean pan through a double thickness of paper towel placed in a sieve.

3 Add prawns and bring mixture to a simmer. Continue cooking until prawns have turned pink; this will only take a few minutes. Remove from heat, add coriander, spring onion, chilli, fish sauce and lime juice. Serve at once.

COOK'S FILE

Storage time: Cook this dish just before serving.

1

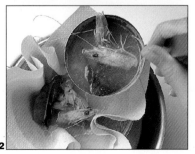

2

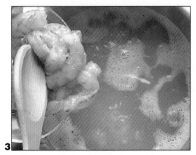

3

STUFFED CHICKEN WINGS

Preparation time: 40 minutes
Cooking time: 20 minutes
Serves 6 as an entrée

6 large chicken wings

Filling
3 tablespoons chopped water
  chestnuts
½ teaspoon finely chopped
  garlic
1 tablespoon finely chopped
  fresh coriander leaves
6 teaspoons fish sauce
½ teaspoon ground black
  pepper
1 spring onion, finely chopped
250 g minced pork
finely shredded raw cabbage, to
  serve

➤ WASH CHICKEN under cold
water. Pat dry with absorbent paper.
1 To bone chicken wings, use a small,
sharp knife. Starting at the drumstick
end, slip the knife down the sides of
the bone, all the way to the joint,
taking care not to pierce the skin. Snap
the bone free.
Start on the next joint with the point
of the knife, taking care not to pierce
the 'elbow'.
2 Once the first part of these two
bones has been freed, the bones can be
pulled out and cut at the knuckle to
release. Reshape the wings.
3 To make the Filling: Combine
the water chestnuts, garlic, coriander
leaves, fish sauce, pepper, spring onion
and pork, mixing thoroughly. Using a
teaspoon, stuff the wings evenly with
Filling, taking care not to overfill or
they will burst during cooking.
4 Place wings on a lightly oiled
steamer, cover and steam over briskly
boiling water for 10 minutes. Transfer
wings to a cold, lightly oiled grill tray;
cook chicken under a moderate heat
for 5 minutes on each side or until
brown and cooked through. Serve on a
bed of cabbage.

COOK'S FILE

Storage time: Cook 1 day ahead and
store, covered, in the refrigerator.
Serve cold.

PORK AND CRAB ROLLS

Preparation time: 40 minutes
Cooking time: 25 minutes
Makes about 30

30 g bean starch noodles
200 g minced pork
200 g crab sticks, flaked
1 large carrot, grated
1 small red onion, finely
   chopped
3 spring onions, finely
   chopped
1 tablespoon fish sauce
½ teaspoon ground black
   pepper
1 x 250 g packet spring roll
   wrappers
oil for deep-frying
1 butter or mignonette lettuce

½ cup fresh Vietnamese mint,
   mint or coriander sprigs
1 thin-skinned cucumber, cut
   into 5 cm slices
fish sauce, extra, for dipping

➤ SOAK NOODLES in boiling water for 20 minutes. Combine pork, crab, carrot, onions, fish sauce and pepper. Drain the noodles, cut them into short pieces and add to the bowl. Mix well.

1 Cut spring roll wrappers in halves diagonally. Work with one half at a time, keeping the remaining wrappers covered with a clean, damp tea-towel to prevent them drying out. Place a tablespoon of the filling along the diagonal and form roll into a thin sausage shape, about 6 cm long.

2 Fold in one corner of the wrapper, roll over once and fold in the other corner. Roll up; seal the final corner with a little water. Continue with the remaining mixture and wrappers.

3 Heat the oil in a deep, heavy-based pan until moderately hot; deep-fry three or four rolls at a time for about 3 minutes or until cooked through. Drain rolls on absorbent paper.

To serve, each diner takes a spring roll and places it on a lettuce leaf. A sprig of mint and a stick of cucumber are then added. The lettuce is wrapped up to enclose the filling, and the roll dipped into the fish sauce.

COOK'S FILE

Storage time: Pork and crab rolls may be frozen at the end of step 2. Place on a baking tray and freeze until firm; pack into freezer bags and label. Store in the freezer for up to 1 month. Can be deep-fried from their frozen state for 5 minutes.

1

2

3

CRAB IN CHILLI AND TOMATO SAUCE

Preparation time: 30 minutes
Cooking time: 12 minutes
Serves 2

1 x 1 kg uncooked mud crab,
  preferably live
1/3 cup oil
1 teaspoon minced ginger
2 teaspoons finely chopped
  garlic
1/2 cup tomato sauce
1 tablespoon sambal oelek
1 tablespoon soft brown sugar
1/3 cup water

2 tablespoons finely chopped
  fresh coriander leaves

➤ PLACE THE CRAB in the freezer
for 2 hours, or until totally immobile.
Pull back apron from the underbelly
and snap off. Twist off legs and claws,
scrub them clean. Pull the body apart.
1 Remove the feathery gills and the
internal organs.
2 Using a cleaver or a heavy, flat-
bladed knife, chop the body into four.
Crack the claws with a good hit with
the back of the cleaver.
Heat the oil in a wok and cook a
quarter of the crab for 2 minutes or
until it changes colour. Remove to a
bowl. Cook the remaining crab in three

batches, adding them to the bowl.
Add ginger and 1 teaspoon garlic to
pan, cook gently until pale golden.
Add tomato sauce, sambal oelek,
brown sugar and water. Cook until the
oil comes to the surface; this will take
about 3 minutes.
3 Add the crab and cook, turning, for
8 minutes. Sprinkle with the coriander
and the remaining crushed garlic; heat
through for 30 seconds. Serve with
steamed white rice or noodles.

COOK'S FILE

Storage time: Freeze crab and chop
it into pieces 1 day ahead. Store pieces,
covered, in the refrigerator. Cook dish
just before serving.

1

2

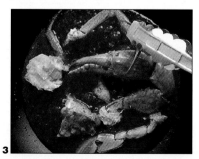

3

MALAYSIAN-STYLE SPICY SQUID

Preparation time: 15 minutes
Cooking time: 15 minutes
Serves 4 (see Hint)

2 medium red onions, roughly
 chopped
4 cloves garlic
500 g calamari hoods or squid
4 tablespoons oil
½ teaspoon shrimp paste
rind of half a lemon, sliced, or
 1 stick lemon grass
2 teaspoons sambal oelek
2 teaspoons tomato paste

1 tablespoon soft brown or
 palm sugar
2 teaspoons lemon juice, malt
 vinegar or tamarind liquid
 (see page 11)
¼ cup coconut cream

➤ PLACE ONION and garlic in a
food processor bowl or blender;
process until smooth.

1 Cut calamari hoods in half lengthways. Holding a sharp knife at a slight
angle, make shallow, close cuts in one
direction across the underside of each
piece; cut in the opposite direction. Cut
into pieces about 4 x 3 cm.

2 Heat the oil in a wok and add the
shrimp paste. Cook for 30 seconds.

Add onion mixture. Cook 5 minutes
over medium heat, stirring, until the
mixture has reduced and the oil has
separated out. Add the lemon rind,
sambal oelek, tomato paste, sugar,
juice and coconut cream. Cook, stirring
occasionally, for about 5 minutes.

3 Add calamari and mix thoroughly.
Cover pan and cook on a low heat for
3 minutes, until the squid is just done.
Serve with steamed or boiled rice.

COOK'S FILE

Storage time: Make 1 day ahead.
Store, covered, in the refrigerator.
Reheat gently over a low heat.

Hint: This is very spicy; serve as a
side dish with other, milder dishes.

1

3

BURMESE CHICKEN CURRY

Preparation time: 45 minutes
Cooking time: 1 hour
Serves 6

1 kg chicken drumsticks or
  thighs
2 large onions, roughly chopped
3 large cloves garlic, peeled
5 cm piece ginger, peeled
2 tablespoons peanut oil
½ teaspoon shrimp paste or
  3 tablespoons fish sauce
  (see Hint)
1 teaspoon salt
2 cups canned coconut milk
1 teaspoon chilli powder,
  optional

Traditional Accompaniments
200 g bean starch noodles
6 spring onions, diagonally
  sliced

⅓ cup chopped fresh coriander
  leaves
2 tablespoons garlic flakes,
  lightly fried
2 tablespoons onion flakes,
  lightly fried
3 lemons, cut in wedges
4 dried chillies, fried in oil to crisp
¼ cup fish sauce

➤ WASH CHICKEN under cold
water. Pat dry with absorbent paper.
1 Place onion, garlic and ginger in a
food processor bowl, process until
smooth. Add a little water to help
blend the mixture, if necessary.
2 Heat oil in pan and add the onion
mixture. Add shrimp paste and cook,
stirring, over high heat for 5 minutes.
Add the chicken, cook over a medium
heat, turning it until browned.
Add the salt, coconut milk and chilli
powder, if using. Bring to the boil.
Reduce the heat to a simmer and cook,
covered, for 30 minutes, stirring mixture occasionally. Uncover and cook

15 minutes or until chicken is tender.
3 Meanwhile, place the noodles in a
bowl, pour boiling water over them
and leave for 20 minutes. Drain, place
in a serving bowl.
Place Traditional Accompaniments in
separate, small bowls. Each diner
helps themself to a portion of noodles,
chicken curry and a selection, or all, of
the accompaniments; the result will be
as hot and tart as each person prefers.

COOK'S FILE

Storage time: Chicken curry can be
prepared ahead of time and frozen.
Cool completely in refrigerator, place
in freezer container and label. Store in
the freezer for 1 month. Alternatively,
make 1 day ahead and store, covered,
in the refrigerator. Reheat over a
moderate heat, stirring occasionally.
Hint: If fish sauce is used, add at the
same time as salt and coconut milk.
Dried garlic flakes and dried onion
flakes are sold in jars at supermarkets.
Fry them lightly in oil until golden.

INDONESIAN CHICKEN IN COCONUT MILK

Preparation time: 15 minutes
+ 1 hour marinating time
Cooking time: 50 minutes
Serves 4

8 large or 12 small chicken
 drumsticks
2 teaspoons crushed garlic
1 teaspoon salt
½ teaspoon ground black
 pepper
2 teaspoons ground cumin
2 teaspoons ground coriander
½ teaspoon ground fennel
½ teaspoon ground cinnamon
3 tablespoons oil
2 medium onions, finely sliced
¾ cup coconut milk
1 cup water
1 tablespoon lemon juice, malt
 vinegar or tamarind liquid
 (see page 11)

➤ WASH CHICKEN under cold water. Pat dry with absorbent paper.

1 Combine the garlic, salt, pepper, cumin, coriander, fennel, cinnamon and 2 tablespoons oil. Rub the mixture thoroughly over the chicken; marinate, covered, 1 hour in refrigerator.

2 Heat remaining oil in a large pan. Add onion, cook, stirring, until soft and golden. Add the chicken and cook quickly over medium-high heat until well browned.

3 Combine the coconut milk, water and lemon juice. Pour over chicken, cover and simmer until chicken is tender and the sauce is well reduced; this will take about 40 minutes. Serve with rice.

COOK'S FILE

Storage time: Cook 1 day ahead.

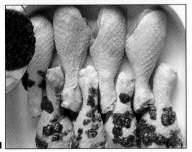

INDONESIAN SPICED CHICKEN

Preparation time: 15 minutes
Cooking time: 1 hour
Serves 6

1.5 kg chicken thighs
1 large onion, roughly chopped
2 teaspoons crushed garlic
1 teaspoon grated ginger
½ teaspoon turmeric
½ teaspoon ground pepper
2 teaspoons ground coriander
1 teaspoon salt
3 strips lemon rind or 3 fresh
    Kaffir lime leaves
1 x 400 mL can coconut milk

1 cup water
2 teaspoons soft brown or palm
    sugar

➤ WASH CHICKEN under cold water. Pat dry with absorbent paper. Trim chicken of excess fat.
Place onion, garlic and ginger in a food processor bowl or blender; process until smooth, adding a little water, if necessary.

1 Place chicken, onion mixture and remaining ingredients in a pan and bring slowly to the boil.

2 Reduce heat to a simmer. Cook, covered, for 45 minutes or until the chicken is tender. Stir occasionally. Remove chicken from pan; remove and discard the lemon rind or lime leaves.

3 Bring sauce remaining in pan to the boil, reduce heat to medium-high, cook, uncovered, stirring occasionally, until quite thick.
Place chicken on a cold, lightly oiled grill and cook under a high heat, browning the pieces on both sides. Serve chicken with the sauce poured over or serve sauce separately.

COOK'S FILE

Storage time: Chicken and sauce can be prepared a day ahead. Store them separately, covered, in the refrigerator. Reheat over a low heat.
Variation: The chicken pieces can be barbecued instead of grilled.
Hint: Store ground spices in airtight containers away from the light.

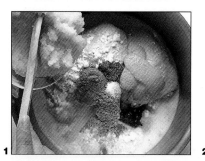

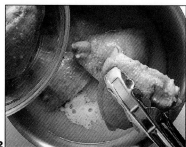

VIETNAMESE CHICKEN SALAD

Preparation time: 40 minutes
Cooking time: 5 minutes
Serves 4

4 lean chicken thigh fillets, cooked
1 cup thinly sliced celery
2 medium carrots, cut into thin, 5 cm lengths
1 cup finely shredded cabbage
1 small onion, sliced
¼ cup fresh coriander leaves
¼ cup finely shredded fresh mint leaves

Dressing
3 tablespoons caster sugar
2 tablespoons water
1 tablespoon fish sauce
1 teaspoon crushed garlic
2 tablespoons white vinegar
1 red chilli, seeded and finely chopped

Topping
2 tablespoons peanut oil
1½ teaspoons chopped garlic
⅓ cup roasted peanuts, finely chopped
1 tablespoon soft brown sugar or 2 teaspoons caster sugar

 SLICE CHICKEN into long, thin strips.

1 Combine the chicken, celery, carrot, cabbage, onion, coriander and mint in a large bowl.
2 To make the Dressing: Combine all ingredients in a small bowl, whisk well until sugar is dissolved and ingredients are well combined.
Pour Dressing over chicken, toss to combine. Place on serving plate.
3 To make the Topping: Heat oil in wok to moderately hot. Add garlic and cook, stirring, until pale golden. Stir in peanuts and sugar. Cool. Sprinkle over salad just before serving.

COOK'S FILE

Storage time: Chicken, dressing and topping can be prepared several hours ahead; assemble just before serving.

1

2

3

MALAYSIAN-STYLE BEEF SATAYS

Preparation time: 30 minutes
    + 2 hours marinating
Cooking time: 8 minutes
Makes 8 satays

750 g rump steak
1 medium onion, grated
½ teaspoon finely grated lemon
    rind
1 teaspoon turmeric
1 teaspoon ground cumin

1 teaspoon ground fennel
1½ teaspoons salt
1 tablespoon soft brown or
    palm sugar
1 tablespoon ketchap manis or
    soy sauce
½ cup coconut milk

➤ TRIM MEAT of any fat and
sinew, slice across the grain into long,
thin strips.
1 Combine meat and all remaining
ingredients in a medium dish.
2 Thread meat on bamboo skewers.
Place in dish with remaining marinade

mixture. Store, covered, in refrigerator
for 2 hours, preferably overnight, turning occasionally.
3 Place the skewered meat on a cold,
lightly oiled grill. Place under a high
heat until well cooked, turning the
skewers occasionally and basting the
meat several times with the marinade.
Serve with rice and a garnish of sliced
cucumber and onion wedges.

COOK'S FILE

Storage time: Meat can be marinated
for up to 1 day in the refrigerator, if a
more intense flavour is preferred.

1

2

3

INDONESIAN DRY BEEF CURRY

Preparation time: 15 minutes
Cooking time: 2 hours 30 minutes
Serves 6

1.5 kg chuck steak
2 medium onions, roughly
   chopped
4 teaspoons crushed garlic
1 x 400 mL can coconut milk
2 teaspoons ground coriander
½ teaspoon ground fennel
2 teaspoons ground cumin
¼ teaspoon ground cloves
4 red chillies, chopped
1 stick lemon grass or 4 strips
   lemon rind
1 tablespoon lemon juice
2 teaspoons soft brown or palm
   sugar

➤ TRIM MEAT of any fat and sinew, cut evenly into small cubes.
Place the onion and garlic in a food processor bowl or blender; process until smooth, adding water if necessary.

1 Heat coconut milk in a large pan, bring to the boil, reduce heat to moderate and cook, uncovered, stirring occasionally until reduced by half and oil has separated out; do not allow to brown. Add coriander, fennel, cumin and cloves, stir and cook 1 minute. Add meat, cook 2 minutes until it changes colour.

2 Add onion mixture, chilli, lemon grass, lemon juice and the sugar. Cook, uncovered, over a moderate heat until liquid is reduced and the mixture is quite thick. Stir frequently to prevent scorching.

3 Continue cooking until the oils from the coconut milk begin to emerge again, letting the curry develop colour and flavour. The dish needs constant

attention at this stage to prevent it burning. The curry is cooked when it is brown and dry.

COOK'S FILE

Storage time: Like most curries, this one benefits from being made ahead of time to allow the flavours to mellow.

Prepare 2 to 3 days ahead and store, covered, in the refrigerator. Reheat over a low heat.
Curry can also be cooled completely in the refrigerator, then stored in a labelled container and frozen for 1 month.
Variation: To get a milder result, remove seeds from chillies.

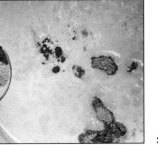

1

2

3

PORK SATAYS

Preparation time: 30 minutes
+ overnight marinating
Cooking time: 8 minutes
Makes 8 satays

750 g pork fillets
1 large onion, roughly chopped
2 cloves garlic
1 stick lemon grass, thick base
  only, chopped,
  or 2 strips lemon rind
2 thick slices galangal,
  optional
1 teaspoon chopped ginger
1 teaspoon ground cumin
½ teaspoon ground fennel
1 tablespoon ground coriander
1 teaspoon turmeric
½ teaspoon salt
1 tablespoon soft dark brown
  sugar

1 tablespoon lemon juice, malt
  vinegar or tamarind liquid
  (see page 11)

➤ PLACE PORK in freezer for about
30 minutes to firm to make slicing
easier.

1 Trim meat of any fat and sinew.
Slice pork across the grain into very
thin, even strips. Place the onion in a
food processor bowl or blender and
process until smooth.

2 Add garlic cloves and lemon grass.
Process until smooth, adding a little
water, if necessary. Transfer onion
mixture to a large bowl.

3 Stir in the galangal, ginger, cumin,
fennel, coriander, turmeric, salt, sugar
and lemon juice.

4 Add meat, stir well to combine.
Store, covered, in the refrigerator overnight, turning occasionally. Drain,
reserving marinade.

5 Thread the meat on long bamboo

skewers. Cover the ends with foil to
prevent burning. Place skewers on a
cold, lightly oiled grill. Cook under
medium-high heat until tender.

6 Turn skewers occasionally, basting
with reserved marinade several times.
Serve at once with Fresh Pineapple
Chutney (see Hint).

COOK'S FILE

Storage time: Cook the satays just before serving.

Variation: A very good result is obtained with grilling, but if a more authentic taste is desired, cook over coals or on a barbecue .

Hint: To make Fresh Pineapple Chutney: Peel one small, slightly under-ripe pineapple, discard tough core. Cut the flesh into 2 cm pieces; place in a bowl. Sprinkle pineapple with ¼ teaspoon salt, ¼ teaspoon chilli powder, 2 tablespoons finely sliced spring onions (green part only)

and 2 tablespoons coarsely chopped salted peanuts. Makes about 1 cup. This is a good accompaniment for curries and rice. Fresh Pineapple Chutney can be prepared a few hours ahead and refrigerated, covered; omit the spring onions and add them just before serving time.

75

COCONUT-CRUSTED LAMB CUTLETS

Preparation time: 10 minutes
  + 2 hours marinating
Cooking time: 10 minutes
Serves 4

12 thin, lean lamb cutlets
1 medium onion, grated
1 teaspoon crushed garlic
1 teaspoon turmeric
½ teaspoon salt
¼ teaspoon ground black
  pepper
2 teaspoons soft dark brown
  or palm sugar
⅓ cup desiccated coconut
2 teaspoons soy sauce
2 tablespoons lemon juice

➤ TRIM MEAT of excess fat and sinew, leaving just a little fat for flavour.

1 Combine all remaining ingredients in a bowl. Stir until the coconut is thoroughly moistened.

2 Add the lamb cutlets and press coconut mixture onto the surface of each one. Cover the bowl with plastic wrap and leave the meat to marinate for 2 hours in the refrigerator.

3 Place cutlets on a cold, lightly oiled grill. Cook under a moderate heat for 3 to 5 minutes on each side, until crisp and golden.

COOK'S FILE

Storage time: A longer marinating time will not hurt this dish. It can be prepared a day or two ahead and refrigerated, covered. Bring to room temperature before grilling.

Hint: Serve with steamed rice or flat bread and side dishes of Gado Gado and Peanut Sauce (see recipes on pages 78 and 79).

CRISP-FRIED THAI NOODLES

Preparation time: 30 minutes
Cooking time: 20 minutes
Serves 6 as an entrée

oil for deep-frying
125 g rice vermicelli
1 teaspoon finely chopped garlic
250 g pork mince
8 medium green prawns, peeled and deveined
2 tablespoons caster sugar
2 tablespoons white vinegar
1 tablespoon fish sauce
1 red chilli, seeded and finely chopped
2 eggs, lightly beaten

125 g fresh bean sprouts, tails removed
2 tablespoons fresh coriander leaves

➤ HEAT OIL in a wok.

1 Use tongs to gently lower small batches of vermicelli into the oil; the strands will instantly swell. Deep-fry each batch of the noodles until golden, turning them to colour both sides. Drain them on absorbent paper. Cool the oil to room temperature.

2 Pour off all but 2 tablespoons oil from wok. Heat the oil, add garlic, stir until golden. Add the mince. Cook over a high heat for 3 minutes until well browned and almost all of the liquid has evaporated.

Add the prawns, stirring for another 30 seconds. Add sugar, vinegar, fish sauce and chilli. Bring to boil, stirring; add the eggs. Cook, stirring, until set.

3 Add the bean sprouts and noodles, tossing them thoroughly to combine. Scatter with coriander leaves. Serve immediately.

COOK'S FILE

Storage time: Noodles can be deep-fried 2 days ahead. Cool completely, store in an airtight container.

Variation: Small pickled garlic cloves can also be added towards the end of cooking to add a sweet/sour flavour.

Hint: Don't attempt to speed things up by deep-frying too many of the noodles at a time; they will not crisp. If still puffed and white, they will not stay crisp when returned to the sauce.

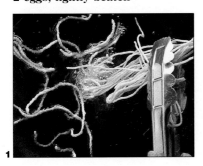

GADO GADO

Preparation time: 20 minutes
Cooking time: 20 minutes
Serves 6

3 eggs
2 medium orange sweet potatoes
2 medium potatoes
125 g yellow squash
250 g cabbage
2 medium carrots, cut into
   1 cm thick strips
1 thin-skinned cucumber
125 g fresh bean sprouts,
   tails removed
watercress sprigs, for garnish
⅔ cup Peanut Sauce (see
   recipe on opposite page)
⅔ cup coconut milk

➤ PLACE EGGS in a small pan with water to cover. Bring to the boil, reduce to a simmer, cook 10 minutes. Pour off hot water, run eggs under cold water to cool thoroughly.

1 Bring a large pan of water to the boil. Cut the sweet potato into 1 cm thick slices. Cut potatoes in half, then into 1.5 cm thick slices. Halve the squash or quarter them if very large. Cut the cabbage into large pieces.

2 Blanch each type of vegetable separately in boiling water; they must be firm and not overcooked. The sweet potato and potato will each need 8 to 10 minutes; the squash, 1 minute; carrots 2 minutes; cabbage 2 minutes. Remove from water with a slotted spoon and plunge into a bowl of iced water to stop the cooking process and set the colour.
Drain vegetables from iced water; dry briefly on a clean tea-towel.

3 Shell eggs and cut in halves or quarters. Slice cucumber into thin strips. Arrange all the vegetables in

decorative groups and garnish with the sliced eggs, bean sprouts and watercress sprigs.
Mix the Peanut Sauce and coconut milk in a small pan, heat through. Serve in a bowl.

COOK'S FILE

Storage time: All the preparatory chopping and blanching work can be done several hours ahead. Do not shell

eggs until serving time. Assemble the whole dish just before serving.

Variation: A strong feature of this dish is its combination of colours and textures. Fresh bean sprouts should be used because they are suitably crisp. If unavailable, do not substitute canned ones which are far too soft; instead, use tender green beans that have been blanched briefly in boiling water. Or, use other seasonal vegetables.

PEANUT SAUCE

Preparation time: 15 minutes
Cooking time: 15 minutes
Makes sufficient sauce concentrate for
  3 cups diluted sauce

¼ cup peanut oil
3 teaspoons finely chopped
  garlic
3 tablespoons dried onion flakes
1 tablespoon small,
  dried chillies
½ teaspoon shrimp paste
1 tablespoon soy sauce or
  ketchap manis
1 tablespoon lemon juice
250 g crunchy peanut
  butter
2 tablespoons raw or demerara
  sugar
½ cup salted, roasted peanuts,
  finely chopped
⅔ cup coconut milk

➤ HEAT HALF THE OIL in a wok.
1 Add the garlic and onion flakes;
cook, removing them to a plate before
they brown as the cooking process
continues after removal from heat.
2 Add chillies to pan, cook until they
puff up and turn black. Chop chillies.
3 Cook the shrimp paste in the
remaining oil, breaking it up with the
back of a spoon. Turn off heat, add soy
sauce and lemon juice. Let sizzle, add
peanut butter, stirring until smooth.
4 Add the onion and garlic mixture to
the peanut butter mixture. Stir in the
chilli, sugar and peanuts. Spoon into a
clean, dry, glass jar, cover and store in
the refrigerator.
To dilute, warm the coconut milk in a
small pan; add about ⅔ cup peanut
sauce concentrate. Stir until smooth.

COOK'S FILE

Storage time: Concentrated peanut
sauce will keep in an airtight jar in the
refrigerator for several weeks. Once
diluted, the sauce should be used
straight away.
Variation: You can vary the amount
of coconut milk depending on the consistency that you require. This sauce
is suitable for satays as well as for
serving with Gado Gado.
Hint: Raw and demerara sugar are
both golden brown and have fairly
coarse granules compared to their soft
brown cousins. They have a definite
caramel flavour.

MIXED VEGETABLES IN MILD CURRY SAUCE

Preparation time: 10 minutes
Cooking time: 25 minutes
Serves 4

6 teaspoons oil
1 large onion, finely sliced
1 teaspoon crushed garlic
1/2 cup peeled and chopped tomato
1 red chilli, chopped
3 strips lemon rind
4 Kaffir lime leaves, dried or fresh
2 teaspoons soft brown or palm sugar

1 teaspoon salt
1 tablespoon fish sauce
1 x 400 mL can coconut milk
1 cup chicken stock
2 teaspoons lemon juice
250 g peeled pumpkin
2 medium orange sweet potatoes
125 g yellow squash
125 g green beans
125 g cabbage

➤ HEAT OIL in a medium pan, add onion and garlic. Cook over medium heat until soft and slightly golden.
1 Add tomato, chilli, lemon rind, lime leaves, sugar, salt, fish sauce, coconut milk, stock and juice; cook 5 minutes until flavour has intensified.

2 Meanwhile, prepare the vegetables. Cut the pumpkin into small wedges and sweet potato into 2 cm pieces. Quarter the squash, top and tail the beans, halving them if long. Cut the cabbage in 1 cm shreds.
3 When the sauce is ready, add the sweet potato and pumpkin and cook for 8 minutes. Add the beans, cabbage and squash and cook for 6 minutes. Serve with rice.

COOK'S FILE

Storage time: Sauce can be prepared a few hours ahead and reheated. Cook the vegetables just before serving.
Hint: Palm sugar is dark, crumbly and robustly flavoured; use the amount indicated or it will dominate.

CURRIED NOODLES WITH PORK

Preparation time: 20 minutes
Cooking time: 10 minutes
Serves 4

125 g rice noodles
1 medium onion
2 tablespoons oil
2 teaspoons mild curry powder
1/2 teaspoon salt
1/2 cup frozen peas
1/4 cup coconut milk or stock

2 teaspoons soy sauce
125 g roast pork or Chinese barbecued pork, thinly sliced (see recipe on page 46)

➤ PLACE RICE NOODLES in a bowl, cover with hot water. Leave to soak for 20 minutes. Drain well in a colander. Cut onion into eighths and separate the layers.
1 Heat oil in a wok and add the onion; cook over high heat for 1 minute. Add curry powder and salt. Add noodles and toss to coat.
2 Add peas, coconut milk and soy

sauce, tossing a few times to combine. Cover wok tightly, reduce heat to very low and cook for 3 minutes.
3 Stir the sliced pork through and heat for a further minute. Serve either as a course on its own or as a snack.

COOK'S FILE

Storage time: Cook this dish just before serving.
Hint: All types of dried noodle must be soaked before cooking; as a general rule, the dry weight will double after soaking. They need only brief cooking. Use egg noodles, if preferred.

Opposite: Mixed Vegetables in Mild Curry Sauce (top), Lightly Curried Noodles with Pork (bottom).

BALINESE-STYLE FRIED RICE

Preparation time: 20 minutes
Cooking time: 20 minutes
Serves 6

2 teaspoons oil
2 eggs, lightly beaten
2 medium onions, chopped
2 cloves garlic
3 tablespoons oil, extra
1/4 teaspoon shrimp paste
250 g raw prawn meat
125 g rump steak, finely sliced
1 cooked chicken breast, finely sliced
5 cups cold, cooked rice
1 tablespoon soy sauce
1 tablespoon fish sauce
1 tablespoon sambal oelek
1 tablespoon tomato paste

6 spring onions, finely chopped spring onions, thin-skinned cucumber, 2-3 long, red chillies, for garnish

➤ HEAT OIL in a wok or deep, heavy-based pan. Season eggs and add to pan.

1 Make an omelette by pulling the cooked edges of the egg towards the centre. When set, turn onto a plate to cool. Cut into fine strips and set aside.

2 Place onions and garlic in a food processor bowl or blender and process until finely chopped. Or, chop very finely by hand, using a sharp knife. Heat extra oil in a wok and cook the onion mixture, stirring frequently until it has reduced in volume and is translucent. Add the shrimp paste and cook a further minute.

3 Add prawn meat and beef to the wok, cook over high heat. Add cooked chicken and rice; toss until heated.

Combine the soy sauce, fish sauce, sambal oelek, tomato paste and spring onion and add to the rice mixture. Mix well. Remove from heat and toss through Spring Onion Brushes. Place on serving platter, add omelette strips, Cucumber Garnish and Chilli Flowers.

4 To make Spring Onion Brushes: Take a 7.5 cm piece of spring onion;

cut a ring of chilli. Thread spring onion through chilli. Make fine, parallel cuts from the end of the onion towards the centre. Place in iced water to open out.

5 To make Cucumber Garnish: Run the tines of a fork down the length of a cucumber and cut into thin slices.

6 To make Chilli Flowers: Take a very sharp knife and make five cuts down the length of each chilli; stop just short of the base. Place in a bowl of iced water for 30 minutes or until the 'flower' opens.

COOK'S FILE

Storage time: Making the garnishes is labour intensive; you can, however, prepare them a few hours ahead and store them in the refrigerator. Cook fried rice just before serving

Variation: This recipe is easily varied to include other types of meat, poultry or seafood that you may have to hand.

Hint: Leftover rice can be used for this recipe, but it must not be more than a day old because it can become sour and unappetising if left too long.

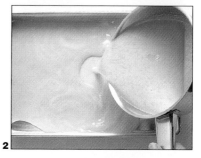

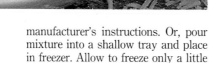

COCONUT CANDY ICE-CREAM

Preparation time: 30 minutes
+ overnight freezing
Cooking time: Nil
Serves 6

Coconut Candy Ice-cream
1 cup water
2 teaspoons gelatine
1 cup caster sugar
1 x 400 mL can coconut milk

Coconut Candy Garnish
2 cups shredded coconut
1/3 cup boiling water
1/2 cup soft brown or palm sugar
1/4 cup water

➤ PLACE WATER in a small pan.
1 Add sugar, bring to the boil, stirring until dissolved. Add gelatine, stirring until dissolved. Remove from heat.
2 Add the coconut milk. Transfer mixture to an ice-cream machine and chill and churn according to the manufacturer's instructions. Or, pour mixture into a shallow tray and place in freezer. Allow to freeze only a little around the edges, then beat to break up the ice crystals. Repeat the process once more before allowing mixture to freeze completely.
Soften slightly before serving. Decorate with Coconut Candy Garnish.
3 To make the Coconut Candy Garnish: Place coconut in a bowl and pour boiling water over. Turn gently to moisten thoroughly. Place sugar and water in a medium pan, dissolve sugar over a moderate heat. Bring to the boil, add coconut. Stir frequently over moderate heat until the syrup has almost evaporated. Reduce the heat to low and stir continuously until the mixture is quite dry.
4 Remove from heat the moment the mixture starts to smell toasted and turns golden. Stir until almost cold, spread out to cool on a buttered baking tray. The coconut candy will be crystallised and sugary when cold. Break into small pieces for serving. Store in an airtight container.

COOK'S FILE

Storage time: The ice-cream can be prepared several days in advance. Coconut Candy Garnish will keep for 2 weeks in an airtight container. Soften slightly before serving.
Hint: Make sure that gelatine is completely dissolved before removing the pan from the heat.
Shredded coconut is sold in packets at health food stores.

SAGO PUDDING WITH SUGAR AND COCONUT MILK

Preparation time: 5 minutes
Cooking time: 20 minutes
Serves 4

4 cups water
½ cup sago
1½ cups coconut milk

½ cup soft dark brown or palm
  sugar
¼ cup water, extra

➤ PLACE WATER in medium pan
and bring to the boil.
1 Gradually add the sago. Simmer for
6 minutes. Cover, leave 10 minutes.
Place in sieve under cold, running water.
2 Pour sago into a lightly oiled bowl,
stir in 2 tablespoons of the coconut milk.
Leave to set at room temperature.

3 Place sugar in small pan with the
extra water. Bring to the boil, simmer
until sugar has dissolved. Strain syrup
into a small bowl and chill.
Unmould pudding onto a serving plate
or spoon it into individual dishes.
Serve the remaining coconut milk and
sugar syrup separately.

COOK'S FILE

Storage time: This can be made a
day ahead and refrigerated.

INDIAN

BEEF SAMOSAS WITH MINT CHUTNEY DIP

Preparation time: 50 minutes
Cooking time: 15 minutes
Makes 20

2 tablespoons oil
1 medium onion, finely chopped
2 teaspoons finely chopped
  ginger
400 g beef mince
1 tablespoon curry powder
1 teaspoon salt
1 medium tomato, peeled and
  chopped
1 medium potato, cubed
¼ cup water
1 tablespoon finely chopped
  fresh mint
1 kg packet ready-rolled puff
  pastry sheets
1 egg yolk, lightly beaten
1 tablespoon cream

Mint Chutney Dip
1 cup fresh mint sprigs
4 spring onions
1 red chilli, seeded
¼ teaspoon salt
1 tablespoon lemon juice
2 teaspoons caster sugar
¼ teaspoon garam masala
¼ cup water

➤ HEAT OIL in a pan, add the onion and ginger. Cook until the onion is soft and golden.

1 Add meat and curry powder. Stir over high heat until the beef has browned. Add salt and tomato, cook, covered, for 5 minutes. Add the potato and water and cook for 5 minutes. Remove from the heat, cool. Stir in the mint.

2 Preheat oven to moderately hot 210˚C. Cut pastry into circles of 13 cm diameter; cut in half. Form cones by folding each of the semi-circles in half and pinching the sides together.

3 Spoon 2 teaspoons of the mince mixture into each cone. Pinch edges together to seal.

Place puffs on a lightly greased baking tray. Beat the egg yolk with the cream and brush over puffs. Cook for 10 to 15 minutes.

To make the Mint Chutney Dip: Roughly chop the mint sprigs, spring onions and chilli and place in a food processor bowl or blender with all the remaining ingredients; process the mixture thoroughly. Serve dip with the hot samosas.

COOK'S FILE

Storage time: Prepare the samosas several hours ahead, refrigerate; Cook just before serving. The dip can be made and refrigerated 1 day ahead.
Hint: Dip can be served as a side dish with many different types of curry. Garam masala is a condiment added to a dish at a late stage in the cooking, just before serving. Sometimes it is used as a flavouring in cold dishes similar to the Mint Chutney Dip.

87

SPICY POTATO SAMOSAS

Preparation time: 40 minutes
Cooking time: 20 minutes
Makes 24

Filling
2 tablespoons ghee or oil
1 large onion, chopped
1 teaspoon finely chopped garlic
1 teaspoon finely chopped
  ginger
½ teaspoon chilli powder
1 teaspoon mustard seeds
1 teaspoon ground cumin
1 teaspoon ground coriander
¼ teaspoon turmeric
½ teaspoon salt
500 g potatoes, cut into
  1 cm cubes
⅓ cup water
1 cup frozen peas
1 tablespoon lemon juice
1 tablespoon finely chopped
  fresh coriander or mint leaves

Pastry
2 cups plain flour
½ teaspoon salt

125 g chilled butter, cut into
  small pieces
⅓ cup iced water
1 egg yolk, lightly beaten

➤ TO MAKE FILLING: Heat ghee in a pan and add the onion, garlic and ginger. Cook until slightly softened.
1 Add chilli, mustard seeds, cumin, coriander, turmeric, salt, potatoes and water and cook 10 minutes. Add peas, lemon juice and coriander and cook a further 5 minutes. Cool.
2 To make Pastry: Place flour and salt in a mixing bowl and rub in the butter until mixture resembles fine breadcrumbs. Add sufficient water to make a soft dough, knead briefly on a floured board, wrap in plastic wrap and refrigerate 20 minutes.
3 Preheat oven to moderate 180°C. Divide the pastry in half. Roll out each half on a floured surface to 3 mm thickness. Cut pastry into circles of 12 cm diameter.
4 Place 2 teaspoons of filling in the centre of each circle, fold over and pleat the edges to seal. Place on a baking tray. Brush with beaten egg yolk and cook for 15 to 20 minutes.

COOK'S FILE

Storage time: Prepare the samosas several hours ahead; refrigerate. Cook just before serving.
Variation: Omit beaten egg glaze and deep-fry the samosas in hot oil for 2 to 3 minutes.
Pastry may also be made in a food processor; process in short bursts to prevent pastry being overworked and becoming tough.

PEA, EGG AND RICOTTA CURRY

Preparation time: 15 minutes
Cooking time: 30 minutes
Serves 4

4 hard-boiled eggs
1/2 teaspoon turmeric
3 tablespoons ghee or oil
1 bay leaf
2 small onions, finely chopped
1 teaspoon finely chopped garlic
1 1/2 teaspoons ground coriander
1 1/2 teaspoons garam masala
1/2 teaspoon chilli powder,
  optional
1/2 cup peeled tomatoes, chopped
1 tablespoon tomato paste

1/2 cup water
125 g baked ricotta cut in 1 cm
  cubes
1/4 teaspoon salt
1 tablespoon plain yoghurt
1/2 cup frozen peas
2 tablespoons finely chopped
  fresh coriander

➤ PEEL EGGS and coat them with
the turmeric.

1 Melt ghee in a pan and cook eggs
over moderate heat, stirring, 2 minutes
to lightly brown. Set aside on a plate.

2 Add the bay leaf, onion and garlic
to the pan and cook over moderate to
high heat, stirring frequently, until the
mixture is well reduced and pale gold.
Lower the heat if mixture is browning
too quickly.

Add coriander, garam masala and chilli
powder, if used; cook until fragrant.

3 Add the tomatoes, tomato paste
and water. Cover, simmer 5 minutes.
Return eggs to pan with the ricotta,
salt, yoghurt and peas; cook 5 minutes.
Remove bay leaf. Sprinkle with
coriander, serve immediately.

COOK'S FILE

Storage time: Cook this dish just
before serving.

Hint: Baked ricotta is available from
delicatessens and some supermarkets.
It is easy to prepare your own. Slice
500 g fresh ricotta, (not cottage cheese
or blended ricotta) into 3 cm thick
slices. Preheat oven to moderately
slow 160°C. Place ricotta on a lightly
greased baking tray; bake 25 minutes.

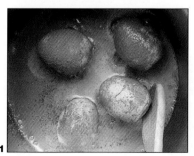

1

2

3

FRIED FISH WITH MILD CURRY AND CORIANDER

Preparation time: 3 minutes
Cooking time: 10 minutes
Serves 4

2 tablespoons ghee
4 white fish fillets, about
   125 g each
1 medium onion, finely chopped
1 teaspoon finely chopped garlic
1 teaspoon ground coriander
2 teaspoons ground cumin
½ teaspoon turmeric
½ teaspoon chilli flakes
1 tablespoon tomato paste
½ cup water
¼ cup finely chopped fresh
   coriander

➤ MELT GHEE in a large pan, add fish and cook for 1 minute on each side. Transfer to a plate.

1 Add the onion and garlic to pan; cook over a medium heat until soft and golden. Add the coriander, cumin, turmeric and chilli, stir and cook for a further 30 seconds.

2 Add the tomato paste and water; simmer for 2 minutes. Add the fish fillets, turning them to coat them in the mixture.

3 Cook 1 minute on each side. When almost done, add the chopped coriander and heat through. Serve with rice or flat breads.

COOK'S FILE

Storage time: Cook this dish just before serving.
Hint: Any firm white fish fillets are suitable for this dish. Cutlets could also be used.

PRAWN CURRY WITH CREAM

Preparation time: 30 minutes
Cooking time: 15 minutes
Serves 4

1 large onion, roughly chopped
2 cloves garlic
1 teaspoon ground sweet
   paprika
½ teaspoon turmeric
3 large red chillies, seeded
1 tablespoon ghee
2 tablespoons oil
1 cup cream
1 kg green prawns, peeled and
   deveined, tails intact
2 teaspoons soft brown or palm
   sugar

Tomato and Onion Salad
1 large red onion
1 large tomato, thinly sliced
salt and chilli powder, to taste
¼ cup fresh coriander or mint
   sprigs, for garnish

➤ PLACE ONION, garlic, paprika and turmeric in a food processor bowl or blender; process until smooth.

1 Add the chillies and blend again until smooth.

2 Heat the ghee and oil in a pan and cook the onion mixture over a medium to low heat until pale gold and fragrant, about 5 minutes.

3 Add cream and bring to the boil. Cook for 3 minutes or until mixture thickens slightly.

Add prawns and sugar. Cook gently until the prawns are just done. Serve immediately with rice or bread.

To make the Tomato and Onion Salad: Cut onion in half and then into wedges. Separate the layers and arrange with the sliced tomato. Season to taste with salt and chilli powder. Garnish with coriander sprigs.

COOK'S FILE

Storage time: Prepare this dish just before serving.
Variation: Use 500 g firm white fish fillets in place of prawns, if preferred. Slice into small pieces.

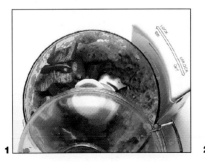

Opposite: Fried Fish with Mild Curry and Coriander (top), Prawn Curry with Cream (bottom).

SPICED FISH FILLETS WITH YOGHURT

Preparation time: 10 minutes
+ 20 minutes marinating
Cooking time: 10 minutes
Serves 4

4 white fish fillets, about
180 g each

3 tablespoons plain yoghurt
1½ teaspoons garam masala
1 teaspoon crushed garlic
½ teaspoon salt
½ teaspoon chilli flakes

➤ PLACE FISH in a large dish.
1 Combine yoghurt, garam masala, garlic, salt and chilli. Spread over the fish fillets; cover, leave to marinate for 20 minutes in a cool place.

2 Drain fish from marinade. Place on a cold, lightly oiled grill tray. Cook under high heat for 2 to 3 minutes each side.
3 The fish should only take a few minutes; it is ready when it can be flaked easily with the point of a knife. Serve with white rice.

COOK'S FILE

Storage time: Cook this dish just before serving.

1

2

3

1

2

3

4

HOT AND SOUR FISH

Preparation time: 30 minutes
Cooking time: 15 minutes
Serves 4

4 white fish cutlets, about
   300 g each
6 teaspoons ground coriander
1 tablespoon ground cumin
¼ teaspoon ground cloves
½ teaspoon ground cinnamon
2 tablespoons lemon juice,
   malt vinegar or tamarind
   liquid (see page 11)
6 tablespoons oil
¼ teaspoon fenugreek seeds
4 dried curry leaves
2 medium onions, finely chopped
3 teaspoons chilli powder
2 teaspoons finely chopped
   garlic

➤ PREHEAT OVEN to moderate
180°C.
1 Cook the coriander and cumin in a
dry pan until medium brown, stirring
constantly. Add cloves, cinnamon and
lemon juice.
Rub the mixture onto the fish cutlets,
coating them well. Refrigerate for 15 to
20 minutes.
2 Heat oil in a large pan; cook the
fenugreek seeds and curry leaves for
2 minutes over high heat. Add onion,
chilli and garlic and cook over
medium heat until soft and golden.
3 Add the fish pieces, only as many
as can make complete contact with the
base of the pan. Sear them on both
sides. Take them out as they are done
and transfer to a large baking dish.
4 Bake, uncovered, for 6 minutes or
until cooked through. Place on serving
plate. Serve garnished with Chilli
Flowers (see page 83) and coriander.

COOK'S FILE

Storage time: Cook this dish just
before serving.
Hint: Fenugreek seeds have a mild
curry flavour with a bitter aftertaste.
They are frequently used in Indian
curries, always in combination with
other spices.
Curry leaves are very similar to bay in
appearance (not taste) and are the key
ingredient in Madras curry powder.

TANDOORI CHICKEN

Preparation time: 15 minutes
+ 4 hours marinating
Cooking time: 20 minutes
Serves 4

2 small chickens (about
750 g each) or
1 kg chicken drumsticks
2 tablespoons malt vinegar or
lemon juice
1½ teaspoons ground chilli
1½ teaspoons ground sweet
paprika
2 teaspoons ground coriander
2 teaspoons ground cumin
1 teaspoon garam masala
1 tablespoon finely grated ginger
1 tablespoon crushed garlic
1 teaspoon salt
⅓ cup plain yoghurt
3 tablespoons ghee, melted,
or oil

➤ WASH CHICKENS under cold
water. Pat dry with absorbent paper.
1 Combine vinegar, chilli, paprika,
coriander, cumin, garam masala,
ginger, garlic, salt and yoghurt in a
large glass or ceramic bowl.
2 Using scissors, remove backbones
from chickens. Turn chickens over and
flatten. Make several slashes in the skin.
Place chickens on a tray, coat well with
the marinade, working it into the flesh.
Cover and marinate 4 hours in the
refrigerator.
3 Place chickens on a cold, lightly
oiled grill. Brush with the melted ghee.
Cook them under a moderately hot
grill for about 20 minutes, turning
them halfway through the cooking;
brush occasionally with any remaining
marinade. Serve chickens with breads
such as naan or chapatis, lemon
wedges and onion and tomato salad.

COOK'S FILE

Storage time: Cook this dish just
before serving. It is also enjoyable cold
and can be stored in the refrigerator,
covered, for 2 days.
Variation: Grilling produces a good
flavour, but for a delicious, smoky
taste, prepare the chicken in the same
way, then cook on a barbecue.
Hint: If you remove the chicken skin,
the flavour of the marinade spices are
able to penetrate the flesh much more
effectively. Also, the finished dish will
contain far less fat than if the skin
were left on.

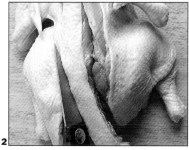

CHICKEN CURRY WITH MANGO AND CREAM

Preparation time: 10 minutes
Cooking time: 20 minutes
Serves 4

750 g chicken breast fillets
2 tablespoons ghee or oil
2 large onions, finely sliced
2 red chillies, seeded and sliced
1 teaspoon grated ginger
1/4 teaspoon saffron strands
1 tablespoon hot water
1/2 teaspoon salt
1/4 teaspoon ground white
   pepper
1/2 teaspoon ground cardamom
1/2 cup cream

2 ripe mangoes or 1 x 425 g
   can mango slices, drained

Mint and Yoghurt Raita
1 cup plain yoghurt
1/4 cup finely chopped fresh
   mint leaves
1 green chilli, seeded and
   chopped
1 teaspoon finely chopped
   ginger
1/2 teaspoon salt

➤ WASH CHICKEN under cold water. Pat dry with absorbent paper.
1 Cut chicken into 3 cm wide strips. Heat ghee in a pan, add onion, chilli and ginger and cook until the onion is soft and golden.
2 Cook the saffron strands in a dry pan over a low heat until dry and crisp, stirring constantly. Cool. Place strands in a bowl; crush with the back of a spoon. Add hot water to dissolve. Add the chicken strips, salt, pepper and cardamom to onion mixture in pan and stir to coat chicken with spices. Add saffron to the pan with the cream. Simmer, uncovered, for 10 minutes.
3 Peel mangoes and slice flesh from the stone. Add to the pan and cook a further 4 minutes until the mango is heated through and slightly softened.
To make Mint and Yoghurt Raita: Mix ingredients together. Serve chilled.

COOK'S FILE

Storage time: Cook 1 day ahead; refrigerate. Because of its fruit content, this curry is not suitable to freeze.

1

2

3

SPICED LAMB RICE

Preparation time: 30 minutes
Cooking time: 2 hours
Serves 6 (see Hint)

3 lamb shanks (about 1 kg)
2 litres water
1 large onion, sliced
10 whole cloves
1 cinnamon stick
5 cardamom pods
1½ teaspoons salt
3 tablespoons ghee or oil
2 medium onions, finely sliced,
    extra
1 teaspoon crushed garlic
¼ teaspoon ground black
    pepper
¼ teaspoon ground
    cinnamon
¼ teaspoon ground cloves
¼ teaspoon ground nutmeg
3 cups long-grain rice
¼ teaspoon saffron strands
¼ cup hot water
currants and shelled pistachios,
    for garnish

➤ PLACE LAMB in a large pan with the water, onion, cloves, cinnamon stick, cardamom pods and salt. Bring to the boil.

1 Skim off any scum and simmer for 1 to 1½ hours depending on the size of the lamb shanks; the meat should be tender. Remove shanks from the cooking liquid, cool slightly. Strain the remaining liquid and measure, adding water, if necessary, to make 5 cups.

2 Heat ghee in a small pan, cook the onion and garlic gently until well reduced and just golden. Add the ground spices.

3 Remove meat from shanks and cut into cubes. Place in a bowl with the onion and spice mixture.

4 Wash and drain the rice. Place half of it in a large pan with a well-fitting lid and cover with the onion and lamb mixture. Place remaining rice on top. Cook the saffron strands in a dry pan over a low heat until dry and crisp, stirring constantly. Cool. Place strands in a bowl and crush with the back of a spoon. Add the water and dissolve. Gently pour reserved cooking liquid and dissolved saffron into the pan and bring to the boil. Cover, reduce heat to very low, cook for 20 minutes. Remove lid, lightly fluff up the rice. Serve garnished with currants and pistachios.

COOK'S FILE

Storage time: Cook this dish just before serving.
Hint: This is served as a side dish.

1

2

4

SPICED ROAST LEG OF LAMB

Preparation time: 30 minutes
  + overnight marinating
Cooking time: 1 hour 30 minutes
Serves 6

1 x 1.7 kg leg of lamb

Marinade
1 tablespoon finely grated
  ginger
2 teaspoons crushed garlic
1 teaspoon turmeric
1 teaspoon garam masala
½ teaspoon chilli flakes

2 teaspoons lime or lemon juice
2 teaspoons oil

Topping
2 tablespoons ground almonds
¼ cup plain yoghurt
1 tablespoon honey
¼ teaspoon saffron strands
¼ cup hot water

➤ TRIM MEAT of excess fat and
sinew. Using a sharp knife, make slits
about 5 cm apart all over the meat.
1 To make Marinade: Combine all
the ingredients. If mixture is too dry to
spread, add a little extra oil. Coat meat
with marinade, pushing it well into the
cuts. Cover and refrigerate overnight.

2 To make Topping: Mix almonds,
yoghurt and honey together.
Cook the saffron strands in a dry pan
over a low heat until dry and crisp,
stirring constantly. Cool. Place strands
in a bowl and crush with the back of
a spoon. Add the water and dissolve.
Add to the other Topping ingredients.
3 Preheat oven to moderate 180°C.
Place lamb on a rack in a baking dish;
pour a little water in the bottom. Bake
for 30 minutes. Spread with Topping,
cook 1 hour for medium; 1½ hours for
well done. Leave 15 minutes; carve.

COOK'S FILE

Storage time: Cook this dish just
before serving.

1

2

3

LAMB KORMA

Preparation time: 15 minutes
Cooking time: 1 hour
Serves 4

1 kg leg of lamb, boned
2 large onions, chopped
2 teaspoons grated ginger
3 teaspoons chopped garlic
3 large dried chillies, or to taste
3 tablespoons ghee or oil
¾ teaspoon turmeric
2 teaspoons ground cumin
3 teaspoons ground coriander
½ cup tomatoes, peeled and
    chopped
¼ teaspoon ground cloves
½ teaspoon ground cinnamon
¼ teaspoon ground cardamom
¼ teaspoon ground black
    pepper

⅓ cup water
½ cup cream

Onion and Mint in Yoghurt
1 medium white onion, very
    finely sliced
2 tablespoons white vinegar
¼ teaspoon salt
1 tablespoon coarsely chopped
    fresh mint
2 tablespoons plain yoghurt

➤ TRIM FAT and sinew from lamb.
1 Cut lamb in 3 cm cubes and set
aside. Place the onion, ginger, garlic
and chillies in a food processor bowl
or blender and process until smooth.
Add a little water to make blending
easier, if necessary.
2 Heat the ghee or oil in a pan and
add the onion mixture. Add the
turmeric, cumin and coriander and
cook, stirring, until the moisture has

evaporated and the mixture has a rich
appearance. Add the meat and stir
over high heat until browned all over.
3 Reduce heat, add the remaining ingredients and simmer gently, covered,
for 30 to 40 minutes. Stir occasionally
to prevent the mixture sticking to the
base of the pan.
Serve with steamed long-grain rice
and Onion and Mint in Yoghurt.
**To make Onion and Mint in
Yoghurt:** Place the onion in a small
glass or ceramic bowl. Pour on the
vinegar and leave for 30 minutes.
Drain off the vinegar and rinse onion
twice in cold water. Drain well; add the
salt, mint and yoghurt. Refrigerate.
Serve well chilled.

COOK'S FILE

Storage time: Cook 3 days ahead
and refrigerate. This dish can also be
frozen for up to 1 month.

1

3

POT-ROASTED BEEF CURRY

Preparation time: 30 minutes
Cooking time: 2 hours
Serves 6

6 teaspoons ground coriander
1 tablespoon ground cumin
1/2 teaspoon ground cloves
12 cardamom pods
2 cinnamon sticks
1 teaspoon turmeric
1/2 teaspoon salt
2 tablespoons ghee
1 tablespoon oil
3 medium onions, finely
  chopped
1 tablespoon finely chopped
  garlic
1 tablespoon finely chopped
  ginger
1.5 kg boneless blade steak, in
  one piece
1/2 cup white vinegar
1 x 400 mL can coconut milk
2 cups water
4 Thai lime leaves or 2 sticks
  lemon grass or 4 strips
  lemon rind
6 teaspoons soft brown or palm
  sugar
2 red chillies, sliced
1/2 cup coconut milk, extra

➤ PLACE CORIANDER in a small, dry pan over medium heat.
1 Cook, stirring, until a deep golden brown and very aromatic. Set aside in a small bowl. Repeat cooking process with the cumin and add to coriander with the cloves, cardamom, cinnamon, turmeric and salt.
2 Heat ghee and oil in a large pan. Add onion, garlic and ginger and cook until soft and golden. Reduce heat to prevent mixture scorching. Add the

spices from the bowl, stirring to combine. Add beef, vinegar, coconut milk, water, lime leaves, sugar and chilli. Bring to the boil, reduce to a simmer. Cook, covered, for about 1½ hours, until meat is very tender.
3 Remove beef from pan and strain cooking liquid into a bowl. Discard the whole spices, lime leaves and lemon grass; retain the onions, returning them to pan with the cooking liquid.

Reduce mixture over a high heat until thick, about 20 minutes. Return the beef to the pan; add the extra coconut milk. Simmer for 15 minutes to heat through. Serve with plain steamed rice or savoury rice.

COOK'S FILE

Storage time: Cook 3 days ahead and refrigerate. Can also be frozen for up to 1 month.

HOT AND SOUR PORK CURRY

Preparation time: 20 minutes
+ overnight marinating
Cooking time: 2 hours
Serves 6

1.5 kg pork (shoulder or
   forequarter)
6 teaspoons garlic, crushed
1 tablespoon finely grated ginger
1 tablespoon ground cumin
1 teaspoon ground black pepper
1½ teaspoons ground cinnamon
1 teaspoon ground nutmeg

¾ teaspoon ground cloves
1 cup white vinegar
3 tablespoons ghee or oil
3 medium onions, finely
   chopped
½ cup tomato juice
3 red chillies, seeded and
   chopped
1 teaspoon salt
1 tablespoon soft brown sugar

➤ REMOVE SKIN from pork and cut meat into 3 cm cubes. Place in a large glass or ceramic bowl.

1 Combine the garlic, ginger, cumin, pepper, cinnamon, nutmeg, cloves and half the vinegar; add to bowl. Turn meat to coat with marinade, cover and refrigerate overnight. Drain pork and reserve marinade.

2 Heat the ghee or oil in a large pan and cook the onion until it is reduced and slightly golden. Add the pork, cook over a high heat until it changes colour.

3 Add the tomato juice, remaining vinegar, chilli and salt. Simmer on low heat, covered, for 1½ hours or until liquid has reduced and thickened and the meat is tender. Stir in sugar.

COOK'S FILE

Storage time: Cook 3 days ahead, refrigerate. Freeze for up to 1 month.

1

2

3

RICH PORK AND COCONUT CURRY

Preparation time: 10 minutes
Cooking time: 1 hour 15 minutes
Serves 4

750 g pork leg or shoulder
1 tablespoon oil
5 curry leaves
1 large onion, finely chopped
3 teaspoons finely chopped
   garlic
1 teaspoon grated ginger
1/2 teaspoon chilli powder
1/2 teaspoon salt

1/2 teaspoon ground cinnamon
1/4 teaspoon ground cloves
1/2 teaspoon fennel seeds
1 teaspoon ground cumin
3 teaspoons ground coriander
2 tablespoons lemon juice, malt
   vinegar or tamarind liquid
   (see page 11)
1/2 cup hot water
1/2 cup coconut milk

➤ TRIM RIND from pork. Cut pork into 3 cm cubes.
1 Heat the oil in a large pan; add the curry leaves, onion and garlic and cook until onion is soft. Add ginger, chilli, salt and spices; cook 1 minute.

2 Add cubed pork and coat with spice mixture. Add juice. Cook 45 minutes, stirring occasionally, or until moisture has evaporated and meat is cooking in its own juices.
3 Cook, stirring, 5 minutes; the colour will darken and the flavours intensify. Add water and coconut milk; simmer 10 minutes until gravy thickens.

COOK'S FILE

Storage time: Cook 3 days ahead and refrigerate. Can also be frozen for up to 1 month.
Hint: Fennel has a liquorice flavour that marries well with other spices in curry dishes.

1

2

3

DRY POTATO CURRY

Preparation time: 10 minutes
Cooking time: 15 minutes
Serves 4

1 tablespoon ghee
　or oil
½ teaspoon black mustard
　seeds
½ teaspoon cumin seeds
¼ teaspoon fennel seeds
1 large onion, finely sliced
½ teaspoon salt
¼ teaspoon turmeric
½ teaspoon chilli powder

1 small green chilli, seeded and
　chopped
¼ cup water
3 teaspoons lemon juice
400 g potatoes, cut in 2 cm cubes
2 teaspoons chopped fresh
　coriander
2 teaspoons chopped fresh mint

➤ HEAT GHEE in a medium pan.
1 Add the mustard, cumin and fennel seeds. When the mustard seeds start to pop, add the onion and cook until softened.
2 Add salt, turmeric, chilli powder, chilli, water, lemon juice and potatoes, cover pan tightly. Cook over low heat

for about 10 minutes, or until cooked, stirring occasionally.
3 Remove from heat, stir through chopped herbs, cover for 2 minutes. Serve with chapatis or parathas.

COOK'S FILE

Storage time: Can be cooked 1 day ahead without the fresh herbs. Reheat gently, stirring in the fresh herbs just before serving.
Hint: Black mustard seeds are, in fact, a dark reddish brown. Cooking them in hot oil, as described in this recipe, gives them a pleasantly nutty taste. Care must be taken when frying; the seeds can jump right out of the pan.

SPICY CREAMED LENTILS

Preparation time: 5 minutes
Cooking time: 45 minutes
Serves 4

1 cup red lentils
2 tablespoons ghee or oil
1 large onion, finely sliced
2 teaspoons finely chopped
　garlic
1 teaspoon finely chopped
　ginger
½ teaspoon turmeric
2½ cups water

½ teaspoon salt
1 teaspoon garam masala
fresh coriander sprigs, for
　garnish

➤ WASH LENTILS and drain thoroughly.
1 Heat ghee in a pan. Add the onion, garlic and ginger and cook until soft and golden. Add turmeric and lentils, cook 1 to 2 minutes.
2 Add water and bring to the boil, reduce heat to a simmer. Add the salt and cook lentil mixture, uncovered, for 15 minutes.
3 Add the garam masala and cook a further 15 minutes until lentils are soft

and most of the liquid has evaporated. Garnish with sprigs of coriander and serve with rice or breads.

COOK'S FILE

Storage time: Cook 2 days ahead and store in the refrigerator.
Variation: Many different types of lentil can be used instead of red. Red have the advantage of cooking quickly.
Hint: Many, but not all, Indian dishes are cooked with ghee in preference to oil. Ghee is clarified butter, and has a rich, nutty taste. A spoonful of ghee is often placed on the top of cooked pulses to give them a richer flavour and a smooth texture.

Opposite: Dry Potato Curry (top),
Spicy Creamed Lentils (bottom).

PARATHAS OR FLAKY UNLEAVENED BREAD

Preparation time: 30 minutes
Cooking time: 10 minutes
Makes 6

½ cup wholemeal or atta flour
1 cup plain or roti flour
½ teaspoon salt
3 tablespoons ghee
½ cup water
2 tablespoons ghee, extra, for
   cooking

➤ SIFT FLOURS and salt into a medium bowl.

1 Rub in 1 tablespoon of the ghee and enough of the water to form a pliable dough. Knead briefly on a lightly floured board. Roll to a rectangle 60 x 30 cm. Soften the remaining ghee to a spreading consistency and spread over the entire surface of the dough. Roll up Swiss roll-style; cut into 6 even pieces.

2 Pinch the cut ends of each piece of dough to seal in the ghee. Lightly flour the work surface and rolling pin and roll out each ball of dough to a circle of about 15 cm diameter. Dust each paratha with flour.

3 Heat a heavy-based pan over moderate heat and melt a little of the extra ghee in it. Cook the parathas one at a time, pressing them lightly with a clean tea-towel or a broad spatula during the cooking to encourage them to puff up. They should take a little more than a minute on each side.

The parathas can be served in place of rice. Serve them with kebabs or a dry curry and with side dishes of pickles and dips.

COOK'S FILE

Storage time: The dough can be prepared a day ahead and refrigerated.

SAVOURY RICE

Preparation time: 10 minutes
Cooking time: 20 minutes
Serves 4

1 tablespoon ghee or oil
1 medium onion, finely sliced
1½ cups long-grain rice
1 teaspoon salt
3 cups boiling water

➤ HEAT GHEE in a medium pan with a well-fitting lid.

1 Add onion, cook until golden brown; set aside on a plate. In the ghee remaining in the pan, lightly cook the rice, stirring, for 2 minutes.

2 Add salt and boiling water and cook, uncovered, until the water has evaporated sufficiently for the surface of the rice to show. Cover tightly, reduce heat to very low and cook for 15 minutes.

3 Remove lid; fluff the rice with a fork and let the steam escape. Spoon onto a serving plate and garnish with reserved onions. Serve immediately.

COOK'S FILE

Storage time: Cook this dish just before serving.

Hint: Rice is an endlessly amenable ingredient that teams well with most spices. This dish can be served as an accompaniment to many in this book.

VEGETABLE OIL PICKLE

Preparation time: 20 minutes
Cooking time: 30 minutes
Makes 4 cups

2 cups oil
3 tablespoons cumin seeds
1 tablespoon fennel seeds
8 tablespoons black mustard
  seeds
¼ cup ground coriander
½ cup ground cumin
⅓ cup finely grated ginger
¼ cup finely grated garlic
2 medium carrots, cut into thin
  strips
3 large red capsicum, seeded
  and cut in thin strips

4 cups cauliflower florets
1½ cups malt vinegar
3 teaspoons salt

➤ HEAT OIL in a stainless-steel pan and add the whole spices.
1 Stir over low heat for 1 minute. Add the ground spices, grated ginger and garlic, cook for 2 minutes.
Add the vegetables, tossing well to distribute the spices.
2 Add vinegar and salt, bring to the boil. Reduce heat to low, cook, uncovered, for 25 minutes, stirring occasionally to prevent mixture sticking to the bottom of the pan.
3 Wash bottles with tight-fitting lids. Place in an oven at low temperature to sterilise while the pickle is cooking. Carefully remove from the oven.

Spoon in the pickles and cover while still hot. Cool, label and store in a cool, dark place.

COOK'S FILE

Storage time: Pickle will keep for about 6 months; the flavour will intensify in that time.
Variation: Add 6 long, red chillies with the vegetables for a hotter taste.
Hint: Pickles and relishes are a mix of flavours – hot and salty, sweet and sour – complementing and contrasting with the main dishes. Simple yoghurt relishes can be made from virtually any vegetable and herb, and are made in a few minutes. Pickles, however, generally require a long maturation process, and will improve in flavour over a period of several weeks.

CHAPATIS

Preparation time: 10 minutes
  + 30 minutes standing time
Cooking time: 20 minutes
Makes 12

1 cup plain flour
1 cup wholemeal or atta
  flour
1 tablespoon ghee
½ teaspoon salt
⅔ cup water

➤ SIFT FLOURS into a medium mixing bowl.
1 Using fingertips, rub in the ghee until well incorporated. Dissolve salt in water, pour into the flour mixture and mix immediately to form a ball. Knead on a lightly floured board for about 5 minutes to make a smooth dough. Leave 30 minutes in a cool place.
2 Divide dough in four equal pieces; divide each quarter into three to make 12 small balls. Roll out each of the balls to about 15 cm diameter, keeping the others covered with a clean, damp

tea-towel to prevent them drying out.
3 Heat a non-stick frying pan to moderate and cook chapatis one at a time for about 1 minute. Turn and cook a further minute, pressing the edges of the chapati with a clean, dry tea-towel to make them puff slightly. As they are cooked, stack them on a plate and cover with a clean tea-towel to keep warm. Serve warm.

COOK'S FILE

Storage time: The dough can be prepared a day ahead and refrigerated.

*Opposite: Vegetable Oil Pickle (top),
Chapatis (bottom).*

RICH ICE-CREAM WITH MANGO

Preparation time: 5 minutes
Cooking time: 1 hour 30 minutes
 + 2 hours freezing
Serves 4 to 6

4 cups milk
1 large, ripe mango (not canned)
¼ cup caster sugar
½ cup water
¼ teaspoon saffron powder
½ teaspoon ground cardamom
⅓ cup caster sugar, extra
½ cup cream
1 teaspoon rosewater, optional
¼ cup blanched, chopped
  pistachios

➤ POUR MILK into a large, heavy-based pan. Place over medium heat.
1 Stir milk as it comes to the boil, reduce heat to low. Leave milk until it reduces to about a third its original volume. Stir occasionally to prevent it catching on the pan base.
2 Peel the mango and cut flesh into cubes. In a separate pan, bring the sugar and water to the boil, add the mango and simmer 1 minute.
3 Add the saffron, cardamom and extra sugar to the milk mixture, then the mango and its cooking syrup, the cream, rosewater and pistachios. Stir to combine. Pour into a loaf tin and place in the freezer to firm to semi-frozen, removing it and stirring it on two or three occasions. Cover the tin with plastic wrap; freeze the mixture completely before serving. Scoop into small dishes to serve.

COOK'S FILE

Storage time: Make up to 1 week ahead and store, well covered, in the freezer.

1

2

3

CARROT MILK PUDDING

Preparation time: 5 minutes
Cooking time: 1 hour
Serves 6

4 cups milk
1½ cups grated carrot
⅓ cup sultanas
½ cup caster sugar
¼ teaspoon ground cinnamon
¼ teaspoon ground cardamom

⅓ cup cream
2 tablespoons shelled, chopped
   pistachios

➤ POUR MILK into a large, heavy-based pan. Place over a medium heat.
1 Stir as it comes to the boil, reduce heat to low and leave until it reduces to about half its original volume. Stir occasionally to prevent it catching on the pan base.
2 Add carrot and sultanas and cook a further 15 minutes.

3 Add sugar, cinnamon, cardamom and cream and cook, stirring, until the sugar dissolves. Serve warm in small dishes; sprinkle with pistachios.

COOK'S FILE

Storage time: Cook this dish just before serving.
Hint: Indian sweets are often made from reduced milk. A heavy pan and an even distribution of heat for boiling down the milk are important. A heavy, non-stick pan would be ideal.

1

2

3

COCONUT CUSTARD WITH SPICES

Preparation time: 20 minutes
Cooking time: 35 minutes
Serves 6

2 cinnamon sticks
2 teaspoons whole cloves
1 teaspoon ground nutmeg
1 cup water
1 cup cream
½ cup soft dark brown or dark palm sugar
1 cup canned coconut milk
3 eggs, lightly beaten
2 egg yolks, lightly beaten

➤ PREHEAT OVEN to moderately slow 160°C.

1 Place spices, water and cream in a medium pan. Bring to simmering point, reduce heat to very low and leave for 5 minutes to allow spices to flavour the liquid.
Add sugar and coconut milk, stirring until sugar is dissolved.

2 Whisk eggs and yolks in a small bowl to combine. Pour the spiced milk mixture over the eggs, stir to combine. Strain into a jug; discard whole spices.

3 Pour custard mixture into 6 small dishes , each of about ½ cup capacity. Place in a baking dish; pour in hot water to come halfway up the sides. Bake for 30 minutes.

4 Insert a knife in the centre of one of the custards; the mixture should be only slightly wobbly. Remove custards from baking dish. Serve hot or chilled.

COOK'S FILE

Storage time: Make 3 days ahead and refrigerate.

Hint: In the traditional version of this dessert, only ground spices are used. However, the method described produces a far smoother texture.

INDEX

SOUTHEAST ASIAN

INDIAN

1 cm	
2 cm	
3 cm	
4 cm	
5 cm	
6 cm	
7 cm	
8 cm	
9 cm	
10 cm	
11 cm	
12 cm	
13 cm	
14 cm	
15 cm	
16 cm	
17 cm	
18 cm	
19 cm	
20 cm	
21 cm	
22 cm	

USEFUL INFORMATION

All our recipes are thoroughly tested in our test kitchen. Standard metric measuring cups and spoons approved by Standards Australia are used in the development of our recipes. All cup and spoon measurements are level. We have used eggs with an average weight of 60 g each in all recipes. Can sizes vary from manufacturer to manufacturer and between countries; use the can size closest to the one suggested in the recipe.

Australian Metric Cup and Spoon Measures

For dry ingredients the standard set of metric measuring cups consists of 1 cup, ½ cup, ⅓ cup and ¼ cup sizes.

For measuring liquids, a transparent, graduated measuring jug is available in either a 250 mL cup or a 1 litre jug.

The basic set of metric spoons, used to measure both dry and liquid ingredients, is made up of 1 tablespoon, 1 teaspoon, ½ teaspoon and ¼ teaspoon.

Note: Australian tablespoon equals 20 mL. British, US and NZ tablespoons equal 15 mL for use in liquid measuring. The teaspoon has a 5 mL capacity and is the same for Australian, British and American markets.

Ingredients in Grams (Aust. Cups)

	1 cup	1¼ cups	1½ cups	1¾ cups	2 cups
Breadcrumbs					
fine, fresh	60	75	90	105	120
dried	90	115	135	155	180
Cocoa Powder					
	85	105	125	150	170
Coconut					
desiccated	75	95	115	130	150
Flour					
	150	190	225	265	300
Sugar					
soft brown	165	205	245	285	330
caster	220	275	330	385	440
granulated	220	275	330	385	440
demerara	205	255	310	360	410
icing	160	200	240	280	320
raw	215	270	325	380	430

Oven Temperatures

Electric	C	F
Very Slow	120	250
Slow	150	300
Mod Slow	160	325
Moderate	180	350
Mod Hot	210	425
Hot	240	475
Very Hot	260	525

Gas	C	F
Very Slow	120	250
Slow	150	300
Mod Slow	160	325
Moderate	180	350
Mod Hot	190	375
Hot	200	400
Very Hot	230	450

British and American Cup and Spoon Conversion

Australian	*British/American*
1 tablespoon	3 teaspoons
2 tablespoons	¼ cup
¼ cup	⅓ cup
⅓ cup	½ cup
½ cup	⅔ cup
⅔ cup	¾ cup
¾ cup	1 cup
1 cup	1¼ cups

Glossary

Australian	*British/American*	*Australian*	*British/American*
Unsalted Butter	Unsalted Butter/Sweet Butter	*Glacé Fruit*	Glacé Fruit/Candied Fruit
125 g butter	125 g butter/1 stick of butter	*Icing Sugar*	Icing Sugar/Superfine Sugar
Bicarbonate of Soda	Bicarbonate of Soda/ Baking Soda	*Plain Flour*	Plain Flour/All-Purpose
Caster Sugar	Castor Sugar/Superfine Sugar	*Self-Raising*	Self-Raising/Self-Rising
Cornflour	Cornflour/Cornstarch	*Sultanas*	Golden Raisins/Seedless White Raisins
Essence	Essence/Extract		

Manager Food Publications:
Jo Anne Calabria
Recipe Origination: Deborah Solomon
Home Economists — Testing and
Step-by-step Photography: Kerrie Ray,
Tracey Rutherford, Melanie McDermont
Food Stylist: Suzie Smith
Food Stylist's Assistant: Cherise Koch
Step-By-Step Photography:
Reg Morrison

Photography: Joseph Filshie
Managing Editor: Lynn Humphries
Design and Art Direction: Lena Lowe

Publisher: Anne Wilson
Publishing Manager: Mark Newman
Production Manager: Catie Ziller
Marketing Manager: Mark Smith
National Sales Manager: Keith Watson
National Library of Australia

Cataloguing-in-Publication-Data
Includes index.
Chinese & Asian: step-by-step
ISBN 0 86411 304 8.
1. Cookery, Oriental. 2. Cookery,
Chinese
641.595
First printed 1993
Printed by Toppan Printing Co. Ltd,
Singapore